way•find•ing Noun

"The ways in which we orient ourselves in a physical space and navigate from place to place. Or, the process and experience of locating, following, or discovering a route through and to a given space."

When we find ourselves in a new place or are feeling lost, we look for directional signs, recognizable landmarks and more to help us find our way.

Wayfinding is a part of everyday life that helps you know where to go. This navigation method, architectural term, and principle of design takes a cross-disciplinary approach to help people find their way, using a range of systems from visuals to the environment, and beyond.

Our hope is that this career resource will provide you with the landmarks you need to find your way. It can be tempting to move towards a future career or take action without pausing to first learn more about who you are and the qualities you need to thrive in the work you do. Whatever situation you find yourself in, this workbook will give you the resources you need to understand yourself in the context of your personal career development, and give you the tools to communicate who you are to the people with and for whom you work.

Career Wayfinder

Discovering your career through delightfully practical projects

Doubleknot

→	Introduction	06
	Hope-Action Theory	07
	Liminal Space	11
	Mapping	14
	My Career Wheel: Part 1	19
	My Career Wheel: Part 2	39
	Using My Career Wheel	61
	Career Options Wheel	65
	Informational Interviews	69
	Goal-Setting & Planning	73
	My Life as a Book	76
	Vantage Points	78
	Developing My Plan	81
	Conclusion	83
	References & Resources	87

Table of Contents

Preface	6

Starting with Hope — 7
- Common career myths — 8
- Thinking about career — 10
- Liminal space in career development — 11
- Mapping — 14
- A Map of Possibilities — 15
- Stepping Stones — 16

My Career Wheel Part 1: Who I Am — 19
- The Career Wheel — 20
- Who are you? — 21
- Discovering transferable skills — 22
- My Skills — 23
- My Career Wheel: Skills — 26
- My Interests — 27
- My Career Wheel: Interests — 29
- My Values — 30
- My Career Wheel: Values — 33
- My Personal Style — 34
- My Career Wheel: Personal Style — 36

My Career Wheel Part 2: Experiences & Opportunities — 39
- Experiences & Opportunities — 40
- My significant others — 41
- Significant others questionnaire — 42
- Questionnaire responses — 43
- My Career Wheel: Significant Others — 45
- Learning Experiences — 46
- My Career Wheel: Learning Experiences — 50
- Work/Life Experiences — 51
- My Career Wheel: Work/Life Experiences — 55
- Career Opportunities — 56
- Career Opportunities: Expanding my network — 57
- Career Opportunities: Brainstorming options — 58
- My Career Wheel: Career Opportunities — 59

Using my Career Wheel: Gaining Clarity — 61
- Using the Career Wheel as an organizing structure — 62
- Defining My Career Wheel — 63
- My Career Wheel — 64
- My Career Option Wheel — 65
- Exploring a Career Option — 66
- Informational Interviews — 69
- Informational Interview Planning — 70

Looking forward and back: Goal-setting & planning — 73
- The journey continues — 74
- Liminal space: Crossing Through — 75
- My Career Story — 76
- Visioning to gain perspective — 78
- Getting ready to make a plan — 80
- Developing my plan — 81
- Accountability — 82
- Conclusion — 83

Endnotes — 84
- Acknowledgements — 84
- About the Authors — 86
- References & Resources — 87
- Testimonials — 89

Preface

This workbook contains a wide array of resources and exercises for wayfinding.

The first section of the workbook includes some foundational perspectives to consider:

Hope-Action Theory: A foundational framework for considering the importance of self-reflection, self-clarity, visioning, and the ever-shifting influences of the environment.

Liminal Space: A space and time of transition. Many people find themselves in a situation where they are crossing over from the known to the unknown.

Mapping: To support transition, we include mapping exercises to help you better understand who you are and where you are at.

The second section of the workbook introduces the Career Wheel as an organizing structure and provides exercises to help assess and clarify the components that influence career options. For those familiar with the "Career Pathways" workbook, these exercises have been updated, and provide a systematic way to consider personal and environmental influences.

1. Reflect on skills, interests, values, and personal style.
2. Consider the impact of learning experiences, significant others, work/life experiences, and career opportunities.
3. Pull everything together and consider the types of career options these components might be pointing toward.

To conclude the Wayfinder workbook, we have a section called *Looking Forward and Back*. This is where you consider what lies ahead and what you have already accomplished.

- **Liminal Space**: If you are in liminal space, this might be the time to cross over to a more defined goal.
- **My Life as a Book**: Thinking about your life as a book, what you have learned, and what lies ahead.
- **Vantage Points**: An exercise where you have the option to step away from your computer and walk through various aspects of the problem.
- **Make a Plan**: Consider next steps, and how you will keep yourself accountable as you move forward. This is not the end of the story, but it does help define next steps.

Starting with hope

To navigate career decision-making it is important to develop, and be aware of, your sense of hopefulness. More than just good feelings, hope is an ability to imagine a meaningful goal and believe you will see positive results if you take specific actions. Having a sense of hopefulness has been correlated with high levels of job satisfaction and performance, clarity in career decision-making, improved academic achievement, sports performance, increased organizational commitment, confidence, and more!

The Hope-Action Theory is based on human behaviour and organizational management theories. Visually represented in this pinwheel, it provides a well-researched framework identifying seven measurable competencies. When strengthened, these competencies support career planning and how to address challenges with positivity, confidence, and hope.

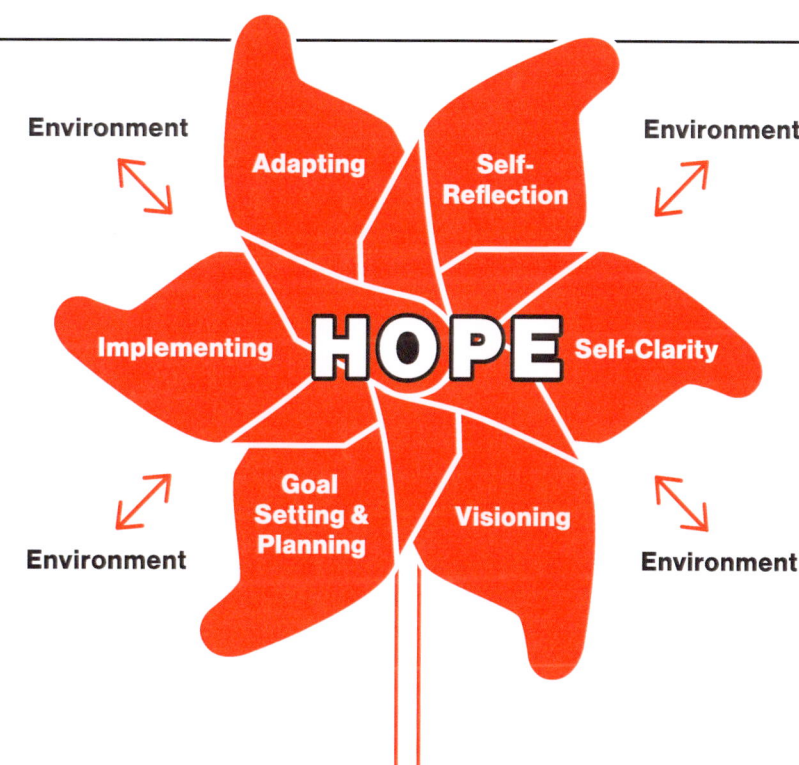

This workbook has been structured with the Hope-Action Theory in mind. As you work through the exercises, you will clarify who you are and the qualities you need to thrive in the work you do.

Before you begin, take a moment to reflect on your levels of strength in each of the competencies, and opportunities for growth.

Want a more accurate picture of your strengths, and some suggestions for how you can increase your hope in specific ways?

Visit **hopeactioninventory.com** to complete the Hope-Action Inventory Assessment.

Common career myths

Thinking about the uncertainty that is experienced in career decision-making can affect how you feel, and your level of hopefulness. It is important to consider what you already believe to be true about career development, as well as the messages others have told you are true.

Activity

Read through the common career myths below and check off any that you believe, or have heard in your learning about career decision-making from the people around you. *Did we miss any?*

○ **I can only be happy in life if I find the right job.**

People often expect their careers to provide them with total life fulfillment. Many people still believe this is possible, but they also know they must look beyond their work. While fulfillment is always something to seek, the workplace is just one area in which to find it.

○ **If I can find a job at a large, secure company, I will be set for life.**

In the past, the right education often led to a job with a secure future. This is no longer realistic. You can make educated guesses about future opportunities, but there are going to be uncertainties. It is important to discover first your interests and abilities, and then look at the current labour market. Look for the opportunities which most reflect who you are.

○ **There are quick courses which will set me up for great jobs.**

People sometimes hope to find a short course that will give them all they need for a well paying job. Although it is true that short courses can be helpful, you should be realistic about what they can deliver and whether or not they will provide you the skills employers are looking for. Take some time to research your options thoroughly when considering courses. You may even need to consider extended skill training.

○ **People only look at my past jobs and education when they decide if they should hire me.**

It is easy to "sell yourself short" by looking at your work or education too narrowly. Expand the way you evaluate past experiences and future opportunities by looking at specific skills and attitudes, rather than just job titles or formal descriptions. Then, learn to communicate your strengths to others in meaningful ways.

Common career myths CONTINUED

○ **Career assessment and planning is something that can be done in two or three short sessions.**

There are some experiences in life that may seem boring or meaningless. You still have to work through these situations and make the best of them. The same principle applies when making career decisions. To reach your dreams you may have to put effort into activities that seem uninteresting or slow-moving (ie. self-assessment, research, etc.).

○ **Sending out hundreds of résumés is the way to begin my job search.**

Résumés are still an important part of a job search, however sending out large quantities of résumés is not the most effective way to look for work. You may feel good when you have done so much hard work, but find that all you receive are rejections, or no response at all. It is better to be focused. Spend time meeting people and researching your options. Go after the most promising opportunities.

○ **My career coach can tell me exactly what I should be doing.**

It is easy to hand over responsibility for making decisions to specialists such as coaches. Even though they can provide some help, you are still the best person to evaluate the options in front of you. Ask questions and seek information from a variety of sources. Trust yourself! You are the one who is going to be living with the results of the decisions you make.

○ **It's easier to choose a career that has the potential to pay well, even if I don't like it. I can enjoy my life when I retire.**

Finding your way to a career that you enjoy and pays well can feel like an insurmountable challenge, but is possible. Pausing to reflect on who you are, and the conditions you need to be able to find fulfillment in the work you do (which is what you will be doing in this workbook), will help you find your way. Career decision-making is a lifelong journey.

○ **There's no point in trying to get anything in this labour market.**

Career planning and job search may be challenging, but do not give up hope; people are still finding work. People are creating new businesses, pursuing further education, and discovering new ways to reach the current labour market. Stay positive and think creatively about your career future.

Thinking about career

As you begin thinking about your career and how you want to engage in the decisions you make throughout your life, it is helpful not only to understand where you are heading, but also to identify what you believe to be true about career. Can you identify any significant people or experiences that have influenced the way you think about your own career growth? The beliefs you hold today have likely been formed out of advice you were given, or possibly your observation of somebody else's experience (positive or negative) in their career.

In the following chapter you will take some time to think about beliefs you hold, as well as the qualities that attract you to the work you do, or hope to do. If you think back to the Hope-Action Theory introduced at the beginning of this workbook, the following series of exercises will give you a small glimpse of your environment and the ways your experiences may be influencing your sense of hopefulness in your career development.

Activity

Before you begin though, see if you can identify at least three things you believe about "career". It does not matter if your answer is "right" or "wrong". Make a list of these beliefs, and the person(s) or experience(s) that may have contributed to them.

_____   _____
_____   _____
_____   _____
_____   _____
_____   _____
_____   _____
_____   _____
_____   _____
_____   _____
_____   _____

Liminal space in career development

Liminal space is a crossing-over, a space where something has been left behind, but you are not fully in something else. It is a space and time of transition. Everybody has experienced, and is currently experiencing liminality, in one way or another.

When growing your career you are often working toward goals, but when you are in liminal space, you may not be sure what those goals are. It can be challenging to look out at the uncertainty that often exists in career conversations and know how to create a vision about what lies ahead for you.

Activity

Here are a few ways people enter into or experience liminal space. Read through the descriptions and check off any you can relate to.

○ **Following your instincts, wanting a change**

　This may be a slower-growing realization (or unease) that emerges over time. You may find it hard to put your finger on exactly what you want, but have a deep sense of something needing to change.

○ **Reaching a milestone and realizing you need something more**

　You may be needing a new challenge. Having a sense of progression or next steps is important, as well as support if transitioning to a new stage of life.

　Not knowing what to do next, or having met all the goals you imagined for yourself early on, can also create a sense of uncertainty and a drop in confidence, particularly if you have navigated your career successfully to this point.

Liminal space in career development CONTINUED

○ **Caught in a changing context, slowly recognizing the need for change**

Recognizing the need for change may cause feelings of loss or relief, depending on your experience. This may be a slow awareness that develops over time, or a quick reaction to a specific event. This changing context may spark grief over what was, or a feeling of being set adrift. Understanding what you need in order to thrive in the workplace (ie. values, skills, personal style, etc.) becomes an anchor to support further exploration.

○ **Experiencing a disruptive event that interrupts life**

An unexpected disruption such as being let go (or fired) can be challenging. It can dampen your sense of hopefulness, reduce your confidence, and even make you feel off balance or out of control. If this is what you are experiencing, we want you to know this is normal. Understanding yourself and the experience of unemployment will help you regain control over your career trajectory and attend to your feelings, so you can move forward when the time is right.

It is also possible that disruption may be paired with an internal desire for change, or a recognition that a change may need to happen. If this is the case, the disruption, although surprising, may be easier to navigate and in some cases, even be a welcome change.

Liminal space in career development CONTINUED

Reflecting back, what career-focused experiences of liminality have you already navigated?

_____
_____
_____
_____
_____
_____
_____
_____

Thinking about where you are today in your career development, what experiences of liminality are you crossing through?

_____
_____
_____
_____
_____
_____
_____
_____

The experience of liminal space is different for everyone.

Your sense of hopefulness can directly impact your ability to effectively engage in your career development. If you are feeling hopeless or frustrated, you may want to reach out to a counsellor or coach to support you in your journey.

Mapping

A common career metaphor is that of a pathway, or a map. Career development tends to involve moving from one place to another, as well as moving across time. Mapping metaphors draw on the Visioning, Goal-Setting, and Planning competencies found in the Hope-Action Theory model, creating a picture of where you are now, and looking ahead to the future steps you might take to help you move from one destination to another. In the following pages you will find a variety of mapping strategies that will help you identify where you are, where you have been, and where you are heading. Knowing this will help you identify strengths, clarify what it is you hope to accomplish in your next steps, move, and better understand your unique experience navigating uncertainty (liminal space) in your career decision-making.

A Map Of Possibilities

On the following page you will find an image of a map. Read over the different locations on this 'Metaphor Map' and think about the following questions:

Where are you now?

_____
_____
_____

Where would you like to be?

_____
_____
_____

How will you get there?
Draw a path that will take you to where you would like to be.

Are there any locations missing?
Draw in any that are missing.

A Map of Possibilities

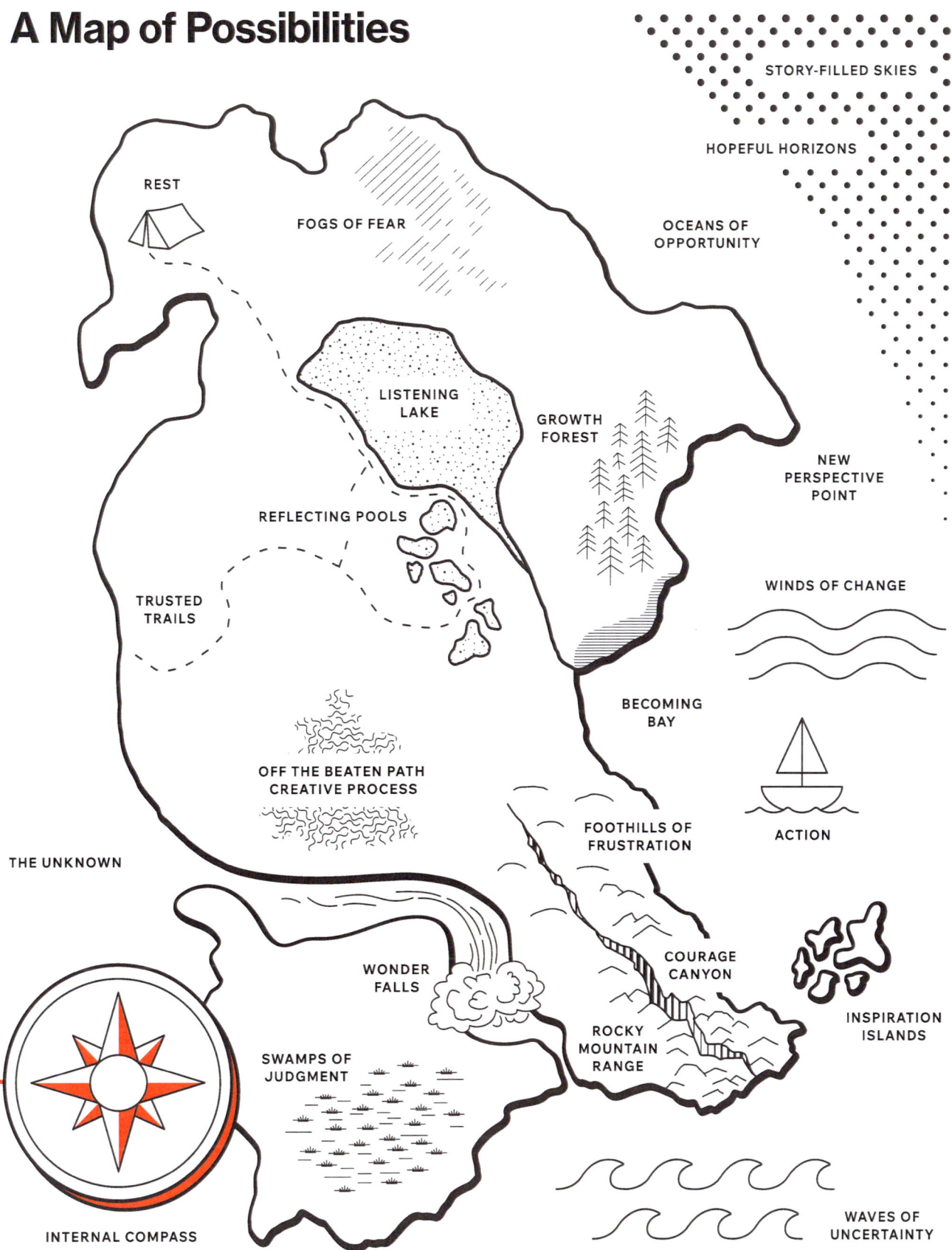

Career Wayfinder 1.0 | doubleknot.works

Stepping Stones

Think of your career journey as a series of stepping stones. You might find yourself leaping from stone to stone, pausing to rest on one as you regain your balance or even standing with your feet spread between two. Career development is never finished; it is a life-long journey of making decisions, moving forward, and sometimes even having to take a step back before continuing on.

There are many different facets to navigating one's career, and it is important to know where you are in order to begin to hone in on the specific challenges you are experiencing. On the following page you will find seven 'stepping stones' that represent the different ways you may be navigating your own career development. As you read over the descriptions of the different stepping stones, pay attention to those that resonate with you at this particular juncture.

My Questions

List the questions you have about your own career growth. Be as specific as you can, to help you narrow in on what you are wanting to understand in your career journey. As you look over your questions, you may find that there are some stepping stones with which your questions will align.

_____   _____
_____   _____
_____   _____
_____   _____
_____   _____
_____   _____
_____   _____
_____   _____
_____   _____
_____   _____

Stepping Stones CONTINUED

Overcoming Barriers — You may not know if you are even ready to start looking for work yet. You need to focus on the challenges in your life before looking for work.

Choosing a Career Direction — You would like to be looking for work but just do not know what type of work or career direction would be the best fit for you.

Learning Job Search Skills — You are ready to start looking for work but do not know how. You may need to learn how to find companies that are hiring, or how to apply and interview well.

Formal Education — You may be thinking about going to school, and wonder what programs are out there, how much they will cost, or how to find the information you need.

Specific Job Training — You may know the industry in which you want to work, but need to upgrade your skills. You may be wondering about mentorships or volunteer opportunities to help you develop the skills you need.

Job Maintenance Skills — You may be wondering about how you can hold onto your work and ensure it will continue to provide you with the income you need.

Career Progression Skills — You may be thinking about how to advance your career. This may mean identifying and pursuing opportunities for advancement, or taking targeted steps to advance your career in another way.

NOTES

01

My Career Wheel

Part 1: Who I Am

The Career Wheel

The Career Wheel is an organizing structure to help you understand your strengths and assets when it comes to career planning. In the following chapters you will complete activities to help you clarify what is important to you within each of the eight segments. Once complete, the career wheel will help you find your way and gain clarity as you make decisions about your career.

Career Wheel Sections

Work & Life Experiences
Notable experiences you have had that helped shape who you are today.

Learning Experiences
Significant past experiences through which you have learned something new. These might have occurred during school, work, volunteer jobs, hobbies, sports, etc.

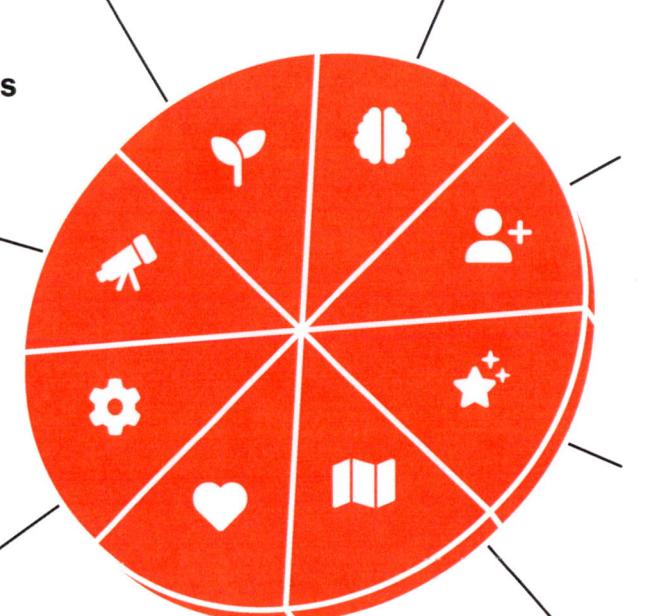

Career Opportunities
Possibilities that are available to you. These may be connections to jobs, opportunities for volunteering, or something else that will help you move forward in your career development.

Significant Others
The people who have, or have had, a significant impact on your life.

Personal Style
How you do things, and the ways you uniquely express yourself.

Skills
A learned ability to do something well. These can be developed in many different ways, in various life situations, or at work.

Interests
The activities you enjoy doing, the subjects about which you enjoy spending time learning, and the things you like in life.

Values
Fundamental beliefs and feelings that guide your actions.

Who are you?

Whatever your experience has been, it is possible for you to take control of your own career growth by putting energy into activities that have been proven to be effective in today's job market.

In this section of the workbook, you will begin gathering information to complete your own personal Career Wheel. As you gather information in each of the sections, you will begin to see a clearer and fuller picture of who you are.

In this chapter, you will be focusing on the bottom half of the wheel. Through a series of exercises you will clarify your skills, interests, values, and personal style. At the end of each exercise you will be asked to narrow down the information gathered, choosing what is most like you, or most important to you. Once you have selected the most important information, you will fill in a section of the wheel as a way of tracking and organizing your assets. We recommend completing these exercises with the support of a coach, counsellor, or career professional.

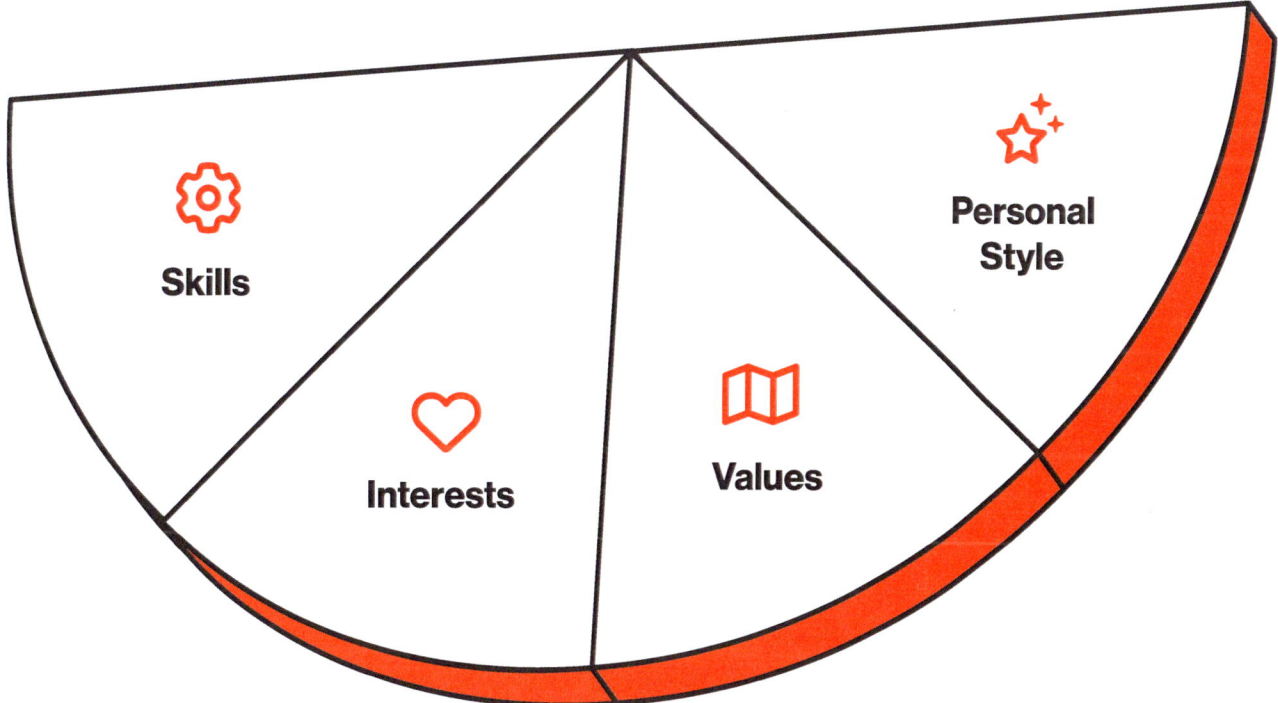

Skills, Interests, Values, and Personal Style

These four sections identify what you can do, how you do them, what is most important in your life, and what kind of person you are.

Discovering transferable skills

What are you good at?

Before making a realistic career plan, you need to know what you are able to do and what you are willing to learn to do.

A 'skill' is a learned ability to do something well. Most people underestimate the number of skills they actually have, which limits their career exploration. This activity will help you gain an accurate picture of all your skills. Knowing what transferable skills you have will help you find career options that will put those skills to use.

One way to discover transferable skills (and more) is by exploring past successes or accomplishments. Use the exercises on the following pages to identify those transferable skills which helped you succeed in the past, and will help you succeed in the future.

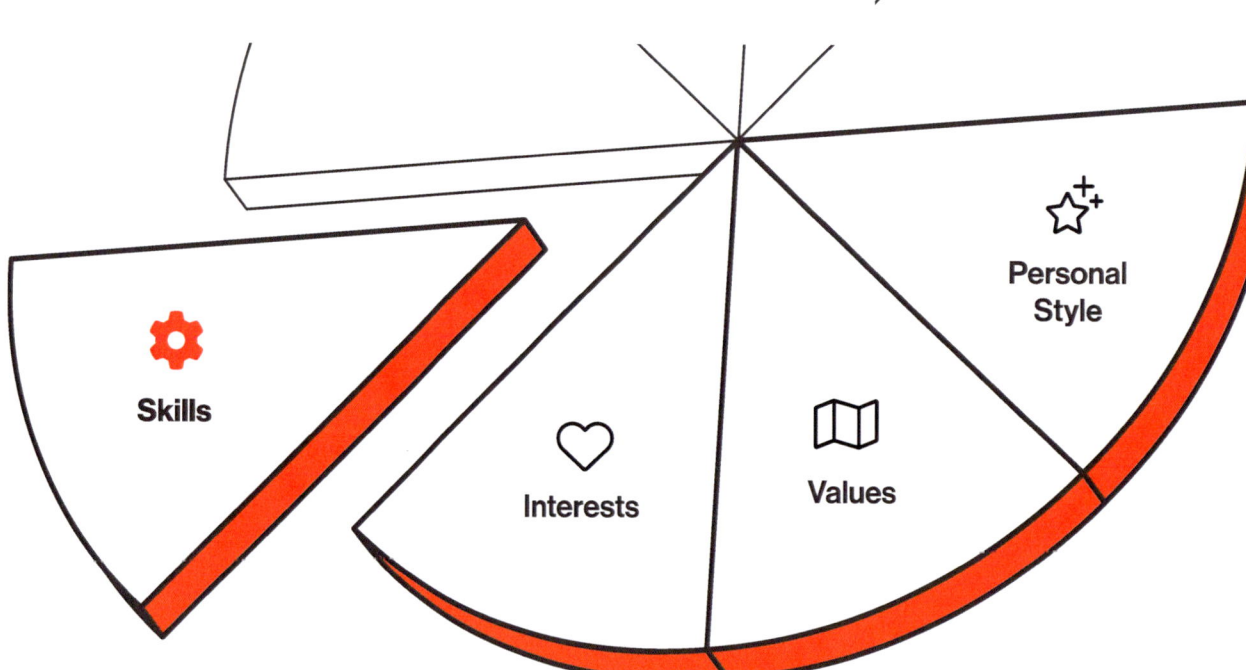

What are transferable skills?

It is important to distinguish between a job title (the name of a specific job), job duties (the tasks done when carrying out a specific job), and transferable skills (the skills/abilities which develop over time that can be used in a variety of situations). A knowledge of your transferable skills will help you expand your career options and help you discover possible careers that use those particular skills.

My Skills

Discovering skills through accomplishments

Accomplishments are past experiences in which you have done well. If you need help getting started, talk with others who know you and ask them to help you identify some of these accomplishments. **Make a list from different areas of your life (volunteer, educational, workplace, hobbies, sports, etc.).**

_____   _____

_____   _____

_____   _____

_____   _____

Expanding The Accomplishment

1. **On a separate page, write complete descriptions of at least two of the accomplishments you have listed above.** Consider the following:
    - What did you actually do?
    - What led up to the accomplishment?
    - What happened after it?
    - How does the accomplishment relate to the rest of your life?

2. Read over your descriptions. Underline any transferable skills directly mentioned in your description.

3. Write down (in the margins, or make a list) any other transferable skills that come to mind.

4. Share your stories with someone you trust. Ask them to suggest additional or related skills you may have overlooked.

Once you have done this initial task, follow the instructions on the following pages to examine your skills further.

You may also use accomplishments as a starting point for exploring your interests, values, and personal style.

My Skills

Check off the skills you already have, and add any other of your skills that are not listed as you go.

Teamwork
- ○ Collaborating
- ○ Taking responsibility
- ○ Listening actively
- ○ Understanding group dynamics
- ○ Identifying strengths
- ○ Motivating
- ○ Giving & receiving feedback
- ○ Cooperating
- ○ Enlisting help
- ○ _____
- ○ _____
- ○ _____

Helping
- ○ Clarifying
- ○ Empathizing
- ○ Coaching
- ○ Mentoring
- ○ Supporting others
- ○ Providing guidance
- ○ Demonstrating
- ○ Listening
- ○ Rehabilitating
- ○ _____
- ○ _____
- ○ _____

Leadership
- ○ Delegating
- ○ Seeing the big picture
- ○ Setting goals
- ○ Planning
- ○ Coordinating
- ○ Problem-solving
- ○ Making decisions
- ○ Implementing
- ○ Building relationships
- ○ Managing projects
- ○ Prioritizing
- ○ Coordinating
- ○ Explaining
- ○ _____
- ○ _____
- ○ _____
- ○ _____
- ○ _____
- ○ _____
- ○ _____
- ○ _____
- ○ _____
- ○ _____
- ○ _____
- ○ _____

Intercultural Awareness
- ○ Promoting fairness
- ○ Recognizing power imbalances
- ○ Examining assumptions
- ○ Respecting individuality
- ○ Asking questions
- ○ Learning
- ○ Self-reflecting
- ○ Navigating cultural differences
- ○ _____
- ○ _____
- ○ _____
- ○ _____
- ○ _____

Communication
- ○ Public speaking
- ○ Organizing information
- ○ Strategizing
- ○ Resolving conflicts
- ○ Negotiating
- ○ Writing
- ○ Learning new technology
- ○ Giving feedback
- ○ Facilitating
- ○ Interviewing
- ○ _____
- ○ _____
- ○ _____

My Skills CONTINUED

Analytical
- ◯ Identifying patterns
- ◯ Understanding metrics
- ◯ Evaluating information
- ◯ Extracting results
- ◯ Developing reports
- ◯ Using databases
- ◯ Collecting data
- ◯ Paying attention to detail
- ◯ Budgeting
- ◯ Diagnosing
- ◯ Planning
- ◯ _____
- ◯ _____
- ◯ _____

Physical
- ◯ Assembling
- ◯ Constructing
- ◯ Following plans
- ◯ Installing
- ◯ Repairing
- ◯ Renovating
- ◯ Operating machinery
- ◯ Cleaning
- ◯ Driving
- ◯ Lifting
- ◯ Being safety aware
- ◯ _____
- ◯ _____
- ◯ _____

Technical
- ◯ Calculating
- ◯ Testing
- ◯ Coding
- ◯ Analyzing data
- ◯ Thinking critically
- ◯ Engineering
- ◯ Assembling
- ◯ Researching
- ◯ Designing
- ◯ _____
- ◯ _____
- ◯ _____
- ◯ _____

Critical Thinking
- ◯ Problem-solving
- ◯ Seeking other perspectives
- ◯ Identifying next steps
- ◯ Analyzing information
- ◯ Providing feedback
- ◯ Advancing new ideas
- ◯ Being objective
- ◯ Synthesizing
- ◯ Strategizing
- ◯ _____
- ◯ _____
- ◯ _____
- ◯ _____

Adaptability
- ◯ Innovating
- ◯ Being courageous
- ◯ Being comfortable with unfamiliarity
- ◯ Trying new things
- ◯ Developing
- ◯ Implementing a vision
- ◯ Imagining alternatives
- ◯ Creating
- ◯ _____
- ◯ _____
- ◯ _____
- ◯ _____

My Career Wheel: Skills

Putting it all together

1. Review the skills you have discovered.
2. Write your top five skills inside this section of the wheel.

Digging deeper

Knowing what your skills are is important. Identifying your top skills will help you begin to gain clarity about your next steps. You will be asked to do this throughout this book. Sometimes this may feel hard, but through this process you will begin to gain clarity about who you are.

It can be easy to get caught up matching skills to work, rather than reflecting on the top skills you possess. Noticing what it was like to identify your top skills can help you learn more about who you are. Was narrowing your skills easy to do, or hard? What can you learn about yourself as you reflect on this experience?

My Interests

When choosing a career direction, your decision encompasses a number of different factors that also influence the way you live your life. As you make your choice, you will need to think about the types of people you want to work with, working conditions, future opportunities, and more. Each occupation tends to have its own unique set of characteristics that go beyond the basic requirements of the job. The more your interests and values align with your role, the more likely it is that you will be satisfied with the work you choose to do.

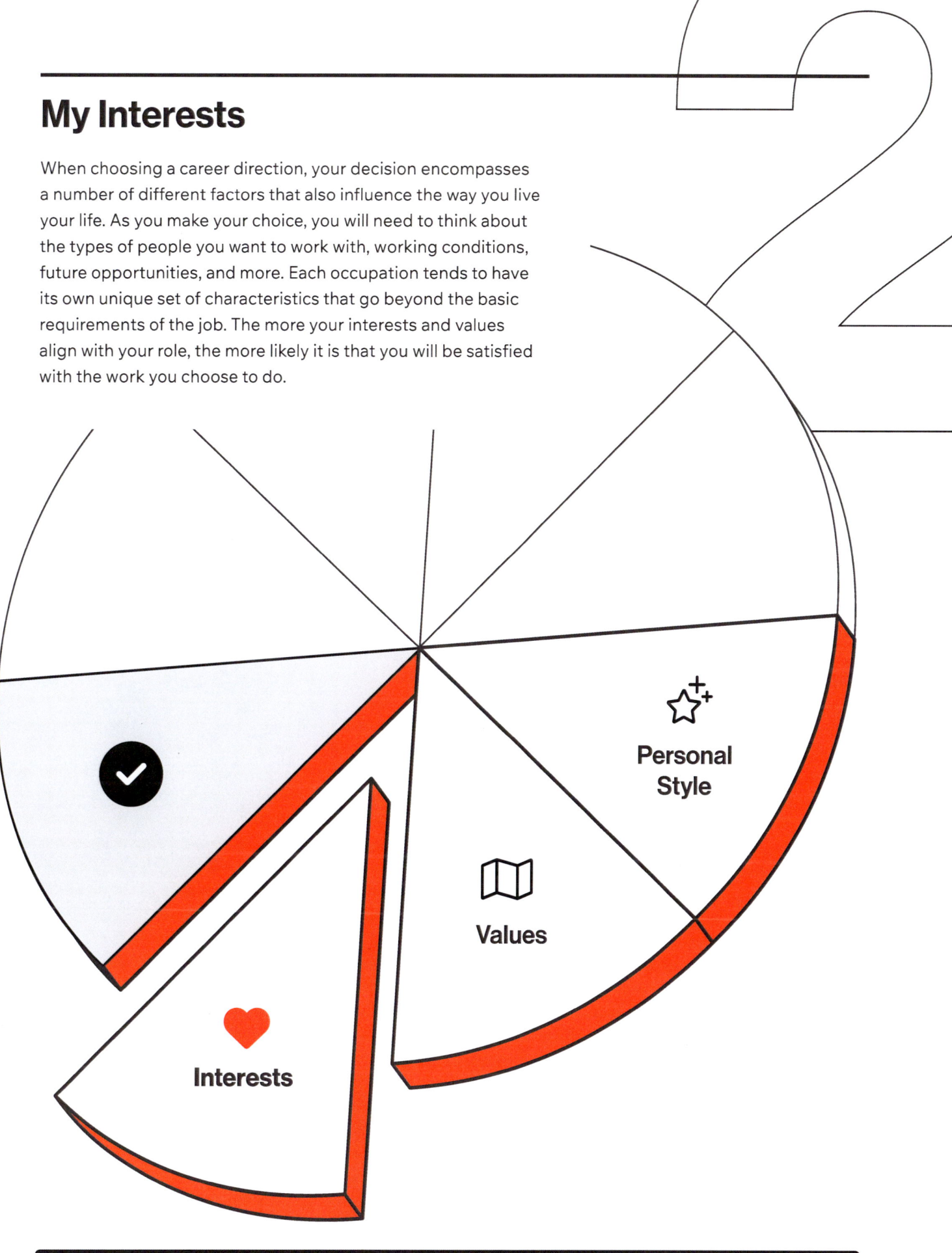

My Interests

When thinking about your interests, it is important to think about all of the different parts of your life, not just your work. The things you do not like can give you clues about what you do like. For example, someone who does not like working on their own probably does like working with people.

My Interests List

Make a list of all of the interests you can think of. Be as specific as you can.

My Career Wheel: Interests

Putting it all together

Write your top five interests inside the section of the wheel below.

Digging deeper

What are some common themes you notice when looking at your list of interests? For example, are they things you do on your own? With others? How do you engage in the activity? Perhaps it requires precision and planning, or perhaps you prefer more flexibility. All of these decisions you make in your day-to-day life can give you clues about who you are, and what is important to you.

My Values

Values are the core beliefs that guide the decisions you make and the actions you take. When thinking about your career, the more your values align with the work you do, the more likely it will be that you find satisfaction in it. Clarifying your values will help you make career decisions, and bring a sense of purpose to your work.

Values can change throughout your life. What was important to you ten years ago may not be so important to you now. Think of the following exercise as a snapshot in time, identifying what is most important to you, based on who you are today.

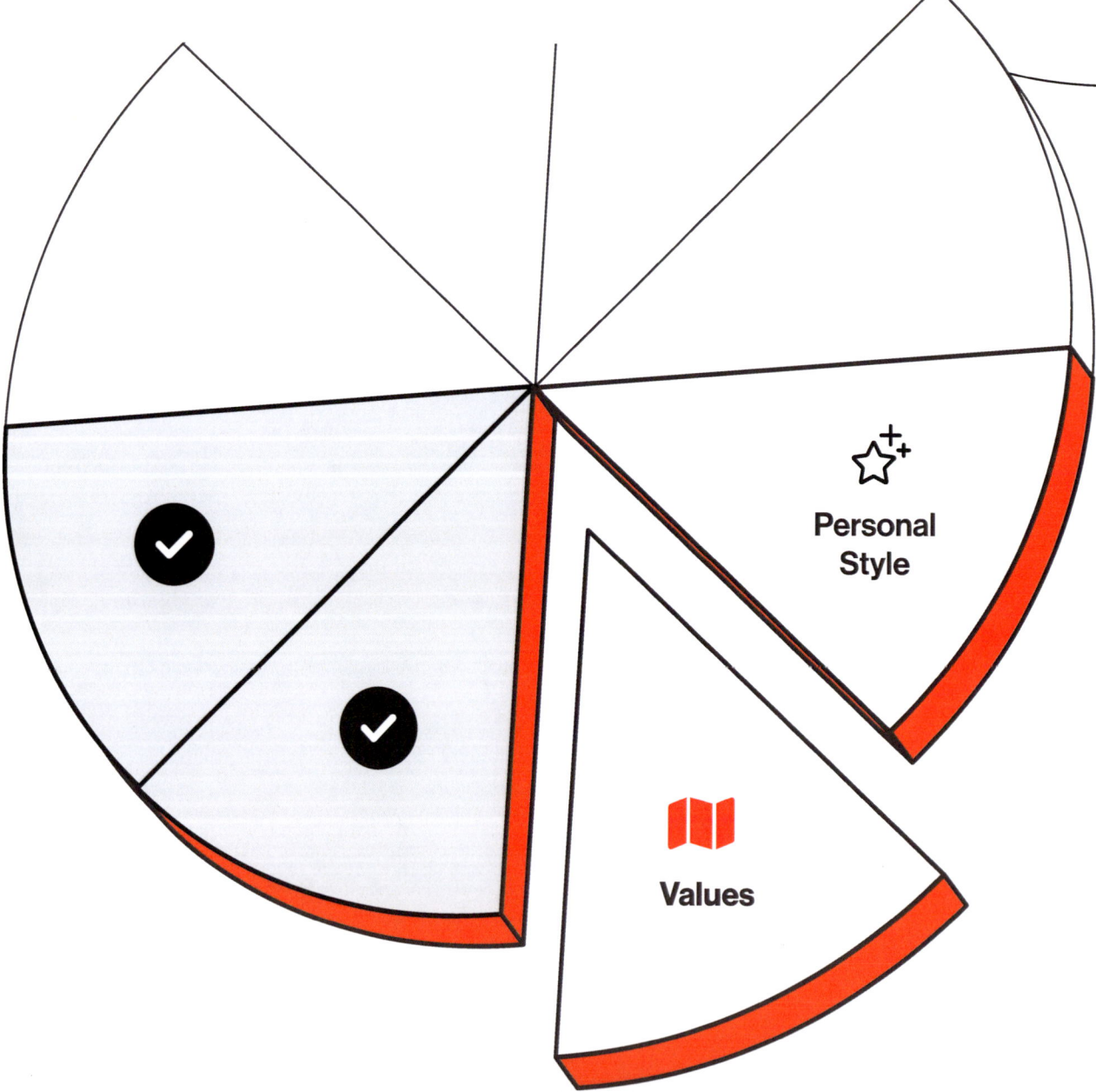

My Values

Identifying your values is only part of the work of gaining clarity and supporting growth in your career journey. It is also important to understand which values are more significant to you than others, as well as those you would be willing to let go of if it meant you could keep the rest. **Read over the list of work-related values below, and on the scale rank them 1 to 5 (1=lowest, 5=highest).**
Did we miss any? Add your own in the space provided.

I Want	1	2	3	4	5
to work and make decisions on my own					
acknowledgement of my accomplishments					
to be challenged, given tasks that require skill and effort					
to take ownership of tasks and be accountable for the outcomes of the work I do					
opportunities to be creative and bring new ideas to the table					
stability and predictability in my work conditions					
diverse tasks, avoiding routine and monotony					
a collaborative and cooperative work environment					
a high income, or to receive financial incentives					
a more flexible schedule					
access to opportunities for continued growth and learning new skills					
to provide guidance and leadership for others in the workplace					
to help and serve others					
minimal supervision when working					
opportunities to be creative and use my imagination					
to impact decisions and outcomes					

I Want	1	2	3	4	5
to understand and connect with others emotionally					
to uphold my moral and ethical principles in my work					
a balance and harmonious integration of my work and personal life					
to contribute to an inclusive work environment					
a dynamic and evolving work setting					
opportunities to innovate and introduce new ideas, approaches, or technologies					
recognition and respect from colleagues					
to find purpose by contributing to the greater good					
to focus on achieving measurable outcomes					
an enjoyable and positive atmosphere at work					
the option to work remotely					
stability and long-term employment					
access to mentorship and guidance					
constructive feedback and guidance about my work					
to do work that positively impacts the community					
access to new technologies in the workplace					
a friendly and supportive work environment					
work that contributes to environmental sustainability and responsibility					
a workplace that values employee health and well-being					
opportunities to work on a global scale					

My Career Wheel: Values

Putting it all together

Now that you have ranked all of the values listed, it is time to narrow down your top values even further. **Choose a maximum of five values that are most important to you, and list them in this wheel section.**

You may want to try the Workplace Attractors card sort exercise available through **doubleknot.works**

This may help you focus in on some of the values that are most important to you.

My Personal Style

It is important to know not only what your skills, values, and interests are, but also your personal style. Your personal style describes how you go about doing things. Understanding your personal style can help others (and you) understand who you are, both personally and professionally. Clarifying your character traits can help you identify the ways you engage in the work you do, which can be useful to know when career planning.

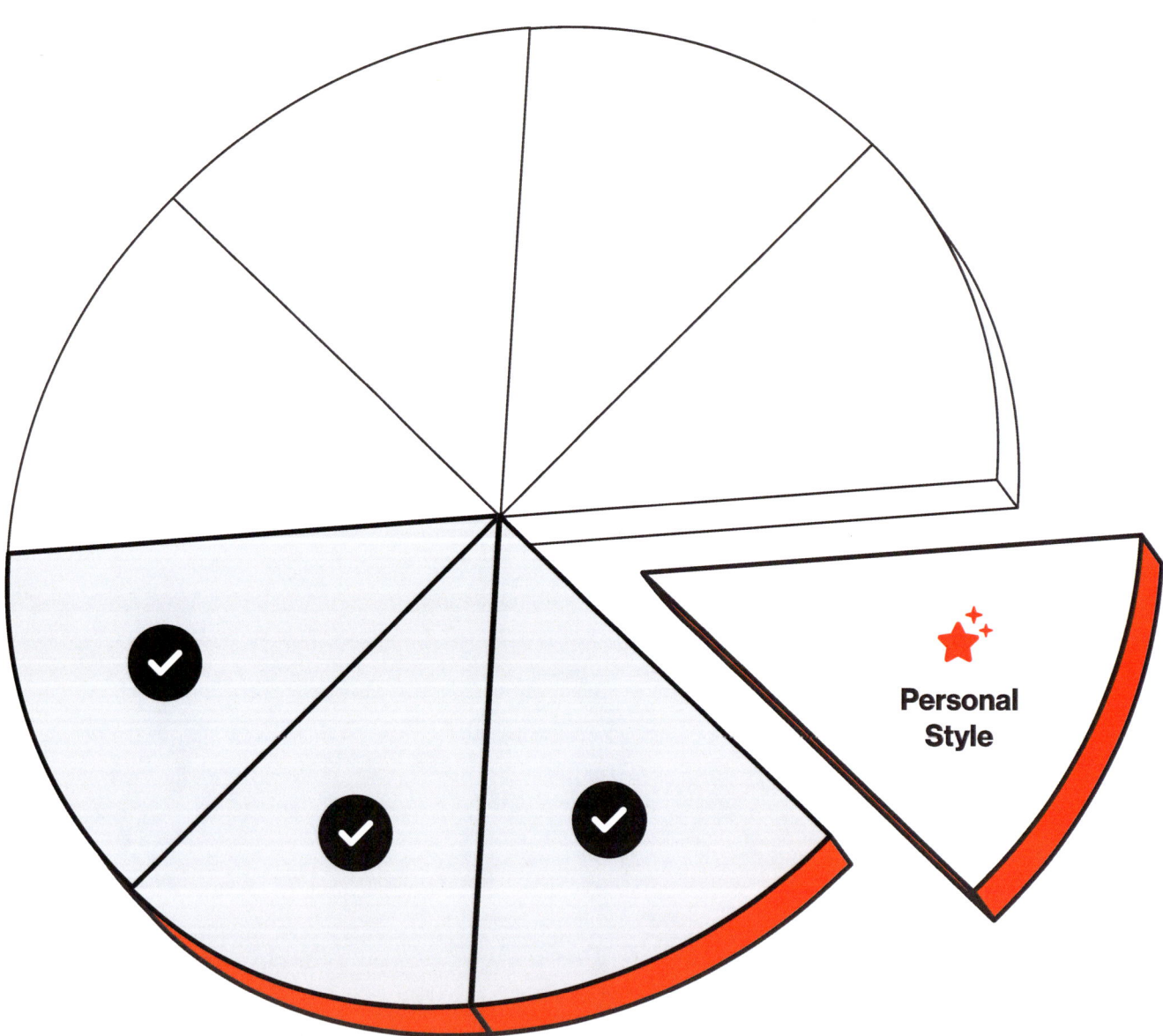

My Personal Style

Personal style describes the characteristics of HOW you do things.

Read over the following list and check off the characteristics you possess. If you have any that are not listed, add them to the list.

- ○ Hard-working
- ○ Trustworthy
- ○ Honest
- ○ Takes initiative
- ○ Learns quickly
- ○ Committed
- ○ Responsible
- ○ Patient
- ○ Shares knowledge
- ○ Extroverted
- ○ Introverted
- ○ Creative
- ○ Thoughtful
- ○ Meets deadlines
- ○ Punctual
- ○ Courageous
- ○ Flexible
- ○ Humble
- ○ Compassionate

- ○ Ambitious
- ○ Conscientious
- ○ Open-minded
- ○ Honourable
- ○ Loyal
- ○ Persistent
- ○ Resilient
- ○ Disciplined
- ○ Agreeable
- ○ Cautious
- ○ Harmonious
- ○ Action oriented
- ○ Outgoing
- ○ Assertive
- ○ Analytical
- ○ Reserved
- ○ Empathic
- ○ Decisive
- ○ Influential

- ○ Positive
- ○ Calm
- ○ Self-confident
- ○ Articulate
- ○ Friendly
- ○ Consistent
- ○ Composed
- ○ Thorough
- ○ Cheerful
- ○ Kind
- ○ Resourceful
- ○ _____
- ○ _____
- ○ _____
- ○ _____
- ○ _____
- ○ _____
- ○ _____
- ○ _____

My Career Wheel: Personal Style

Putting it all together

Write your top five personal styles inside this section of the wheel.

When thinking about your personal style, it can be helpful to ask the people around you how they view you.

The Individual Style Survey is a 360° assessment that can help you understand your personal style as you see it, as well as from the perspectives of the people around you.

NOTES

NOTES

02

My Career Wheel

Part 2: Experiences & Opportunities

Experiences & Opportunities

With the lower half of your personal career wheel complete, this chapter will now lead you through the process of exploring the more externally focused parts of career development. From identifying significant others and career opportunities to naming and developing a better understanding of work, life, and learning experiences, this section will help you be more aware of who you are. As you go through the following exercises, you may come across something that you feel belongs in the bottom half of your career wheel. Go ahead and continue adding to your career wheel, making sure you are also re-clarifying what is most important in each section, if you do decide to make additions or changes.

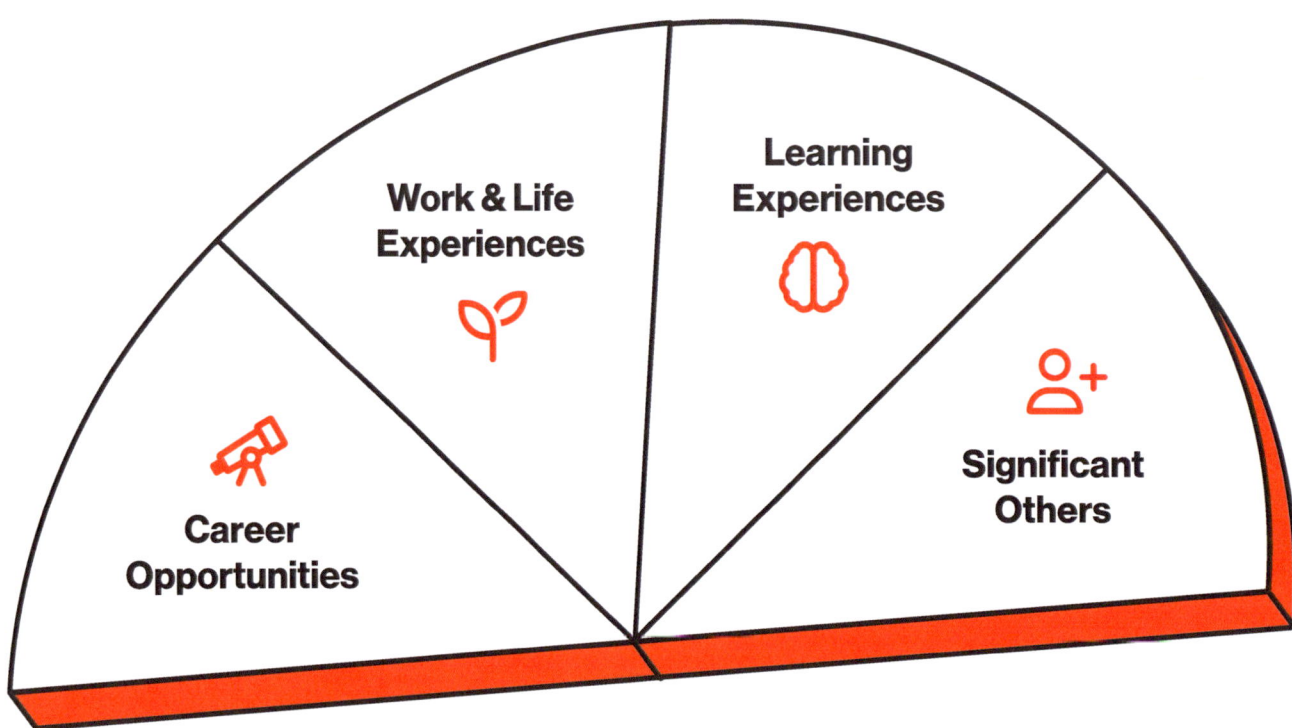

**Significant Others, Learning Experiences,
Work & Life Experiences, and Career Opportunities**

These four sections are the external elements that have helped, and continue to shape, who you are and the career decisions you make.

My significant others

Getting input from others as part of your career development can help you see yourself and the journey you are on from new perspectives. The people around you will help you understand yourself in new ways, and may even spark new ideas and options you have not considered.

When inviting others into the following process, it is essential to weigh the information gathered against what you know to be true of yourself. If you do encounter information that does not align with who you think you are, circle back and ask them to tell you more. Ultimately it is up to you to decide what information gets a place on your wheel. Whether you agree or disagree, by asking for more information you will better clarify who you are, and maybe even learn something new.

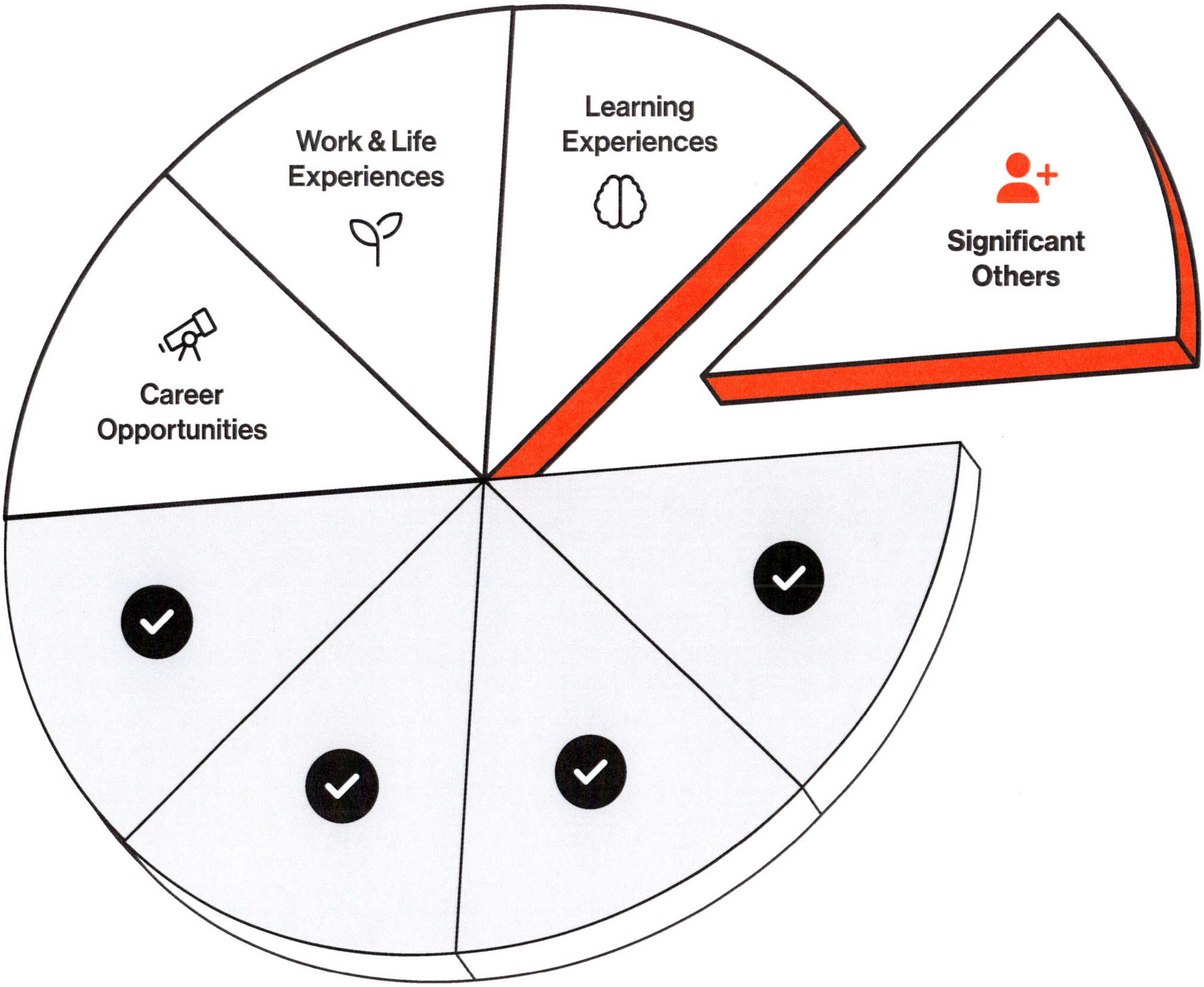

Significant others questionnaire

Identify the people in your life who know you well and are positive influences. These significant voices in your life may be from any part of your system, from family members and friends to colleagues and managers.

List three people you would consider to be a significant other.

Invite each person listed to respond to a series of questions about you. You may want to talk with them directly, send the questions to think about in advance, or invite them to respond in written form.

Below is a list of questions to use as a starting point, though they may not all be the right questions you need to be asking. Spend some time thinking about the questions you want to ask based on what you hope to learn about yourself and your future career. Ask a friend, or your career coach, if you need help.

- What am I good at?

- What are my top skills?

- What do you see as my primary areas of interest?

- How would you describe who I am?

- What positive things have you noticed about me that I may not have seen in myself?

- From your perspective, what could I do more of?

- If you were to suggest an ideal job or career possibility for me, what would it be?

Once you receive responses to your questionnaire, consider the following:

- Is there anything that needs to be clarified, or that you want to learn more about?

- Are there any common themes or patterns emerging?

- What new insights can you gain from reflecting on the responses received?

Questionnaire responses

Review the information you have gathered from your significant others, and consolidate what you have learned.

 STAR ANYTHING YOU HEAR MULTIPLE TIMES

QUESTION
RESPONSES
QUESTION
RESPONSES
QUESTION
RESPONSES

Are there any common themes or patterns emerging?

What new insights can you gain from reflecting on the responses received?

Questionnaire responses CONTINUED

QUESTION
RESPONSES

QUESTION
RESPONSES

QUESTION
RESPONSES

Are there any common themes or patterns emerging?

What new insights can you gain from reflecting on the responses received?

My Career Wheel: Significant Others

Putting it all together

1. List the significant others who most impact your career development, or who are most impacted by your career development, in the section of the wheel.

2. Review the information gathered, review your wheel, and add any additional information gathered to other appropriate wheel sections as needed.

Digging deeper

If you receive responses to your questionnaires that you want to know more about, or are not sure about, go back to the person who responded and ask them to clarify. If you do not agree with someone's perspective, you may find it useful to discuss this with someone you trust, to learn more about who you are, and your response to this information. You do not have to add everything to your book.

Learning Experiences

As you probably already know, learning can happen in a variety of ways. All of life's experiences can be explored to identify what you have learned from them, whether from formal education or not.

Think through past formal learning experiences, as well as roles you have had throughout your life. Learning experiences can be found throughout all aspects of life. Here are some ways you may have been engaged in learning. **Check the ones that you can identify as personal learning experiences, and add your own below.** What is listed is only the beginning; learning is everywhere!

- ○ Volunteer work
- ○ Raising kids
- ○ Sports
- ○ Hobbies
- ○ Workshops & conferences
- ○ Working with a coach
- ○ Being mentored
- ○ Part-time jobs
- ○ Reading
- ○ Previous jobs
- ○ Formal education
- ○ Teaching
- ○ Making
- ○ _____
- ○ _____
- ○ _____
- ○ _____

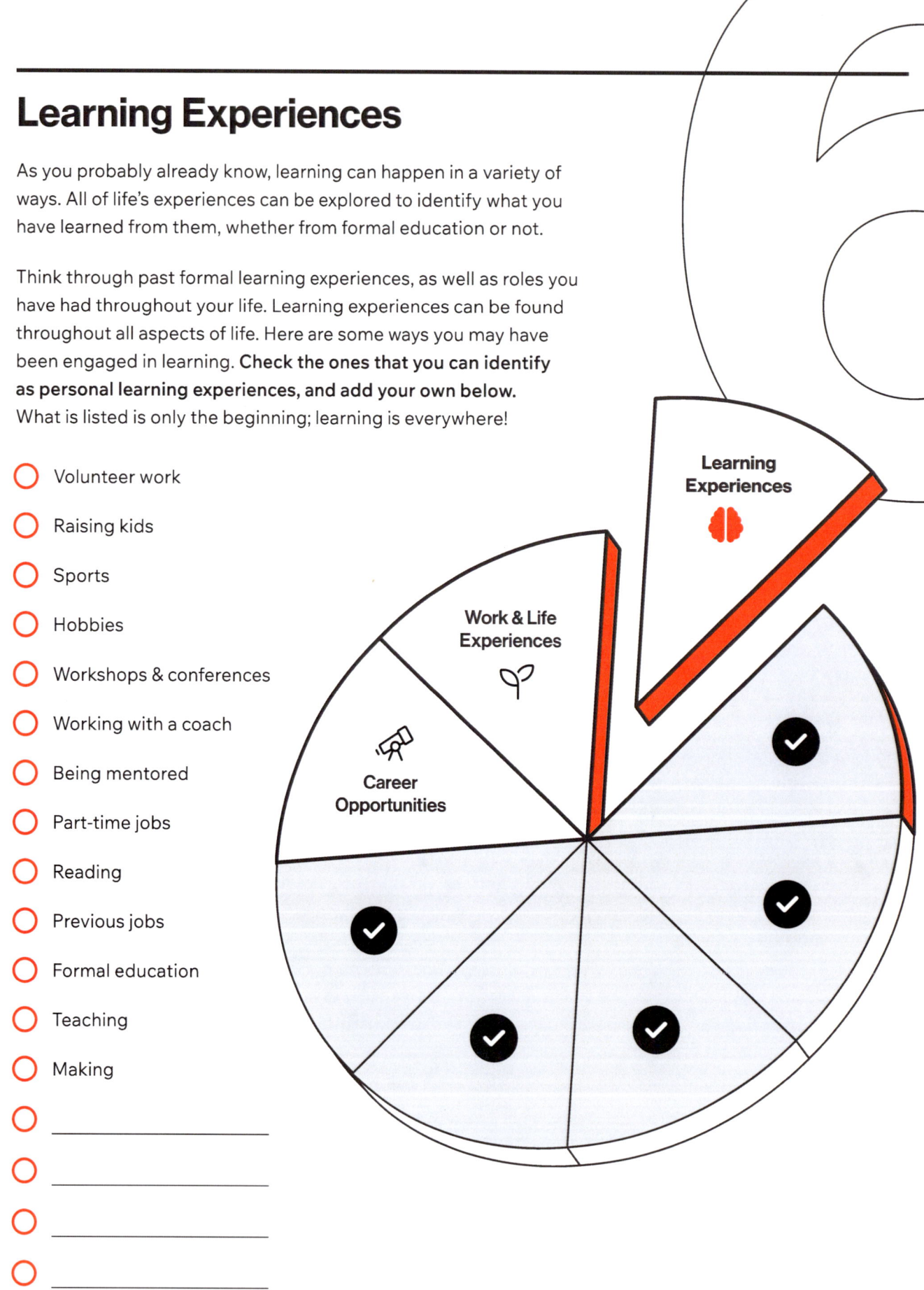

Career Wayfinder 1.0 | doubleknot.works

Learning Experiences 1/3

Choose one learning experience that you would consider to be a success, and complete the following. The more specific you are in your answers, the more you will get out of it. **You will do this 3 times.**

EXPERIENCE	DATE(S)
DESCRIPTION OF THE LEARNING EXPERIENCE	
WHAT I LEARNED	**THE CONDITIONS THAT HELPED ME LEARN**
ACCOMPLISHMENTS (including any special recognition or awards if applicable)	
WHAT I LIKED ABOUT THIS EXPERIENCE	**WHAT I COULD'VE DONE WITHOUT**
PEOPLE I MET (instructors, mentors, learners, etc.)	
WHY THIS EXPERIENCE IS IMPORTANT TO ME	
WHAT I NOTICE ABOUT THE WAYS I LIKE TO LEARN	
ADDITIONAL COMMENTS	

Learning Experiences 2/3

EXPERIENCE	DATE(S)

DESCRIPTION OF THE LEARNING EXPERIENCE

WHAT I LEARNED	THE CONDITIONS THAT HELPED ME LEARN

ACCOMPLISHMENTS (including any special recognition or awards if applicable)

WHAT I LIKED ABOUT THIS EXPERIENCE	WHAT I COULD'VE DONE WITHOUT

PEOPLE I MET (instructors, mentors, learners, etc.)

WHY THIS EXPERIENCE IS IMPORTANT TO ME

WHAT I NOTICE ABOUT THE WAYS I LIKE TO LEARN

ADDITIONAL COMMENTS

Learning Experiences 3/3

EXPERIENCE	DATE(S)

DESCRIPTION OF THE LEARNING EXPERIENCE

WHAT I LEARNED	THE CONDITIONS THAT HELPED ME LEARN

ACCOMPLISHMENTS   (including any special recognition or awards if applicable)

WHAT I LIKED ABOUT THIS EXPERIENCE	WHAT I COULD'VE DONE WITHOUT

PEOPLE I MET   (instructors, mentors, learners, etc.)

WHY THIS EXPERIENCE IS IMPORTANT TO ME

WHAT I NOTICE ABOUT THE WAYS I LIKE TO LEARN

ADDITIONAL COMMENTS

My Career Wheel: Learning Experiences

Putting it all together

List your top three learning experiences on this wheel section.

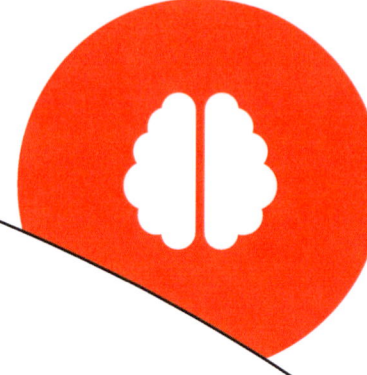

Digging deeper

Looking at your top learning experiences, think about one that was a highlight for you. What patterns can you identify that might give you more information about how you like to learn? Pay attention to the conditions you were in that created this positive experience.

Work/Life Experiences

Reflecting on the jobs you have had is something most people are aware of needing to do. It is good to remember to not only focus on previous work experiences, but to also spend time examining the experiences you have had throughout your life as a whole.

In the following pages you will have an opportunity to identify and unpack your key work and life experiences, using your past to learn more about who you are. As you identify and explore specific experiences, keep a broad perspective. Try to notice any patterns that may emerge, or that might indicate what is most important to you in future career planning. You may even identify something significant that can be added to one of the previous sections of the wheel (skills, interests, values, etc.).

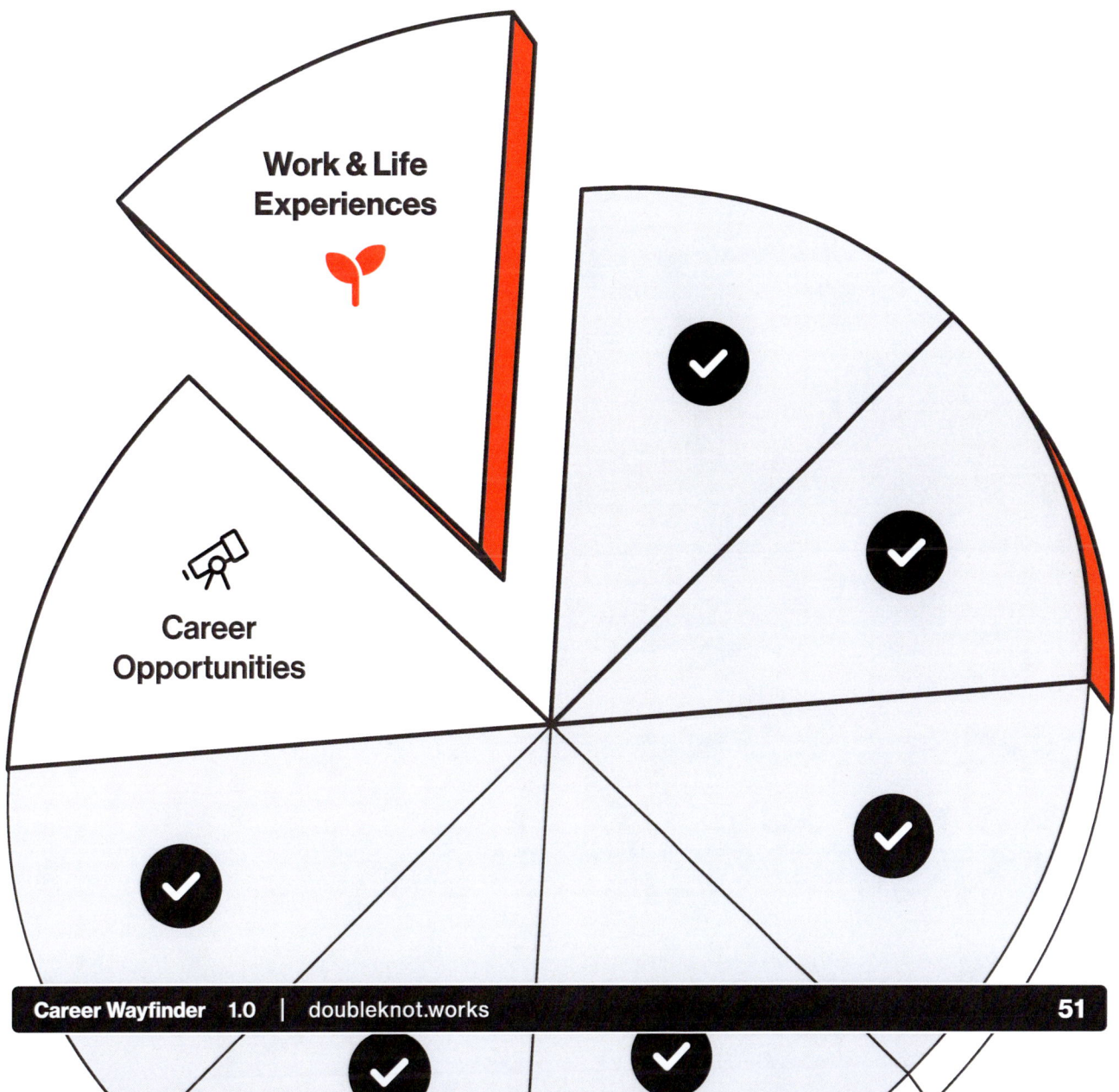

Work/Life Experiences 1/3

Choose one work or life experience that you would consider to be a success, and complete the following. The more specific you are in your answers, the more you will get out of it. **You will do this three times.**

EXPERIENCE	DATE(S)
BRIEF DESCRIPTION OF THE EXPERIENCE	
ACCOMPLISHMENTS (including any special recognition or awards if applicable)	

ONE CHALLENGE I HAD TO NAVIGATE	WHAT I LIKED ABOUT THIS EXPERIENCE
WHAT I COULD'VE DONE WITHOUT	**PERSONAL CHARACTERISTICS AND STRENGTHS I DREW ON**

PEOPLE I WORKED WITH (Place a ⊕ for a positive relationship, ⊖ for a negative relationship, or leave blank)

IF I COULD GO BACK IN TIME AND DO ONE THING DIFFERENTLY, IT WOULD BE…

ADDITIONAL COMMENTS

Work/Life Experiences 2/3

EXPERIENCE	DATE(S)

BRIEF DESCRIPTION OF THE EXPERIENCE

ACCOMPLISHMENTS (including any special recognition or awards if applicable)

ONE CHALLENGE I HAD TO NAVIGATE	WHAT I LIKED ABOUT THIS EXPERIENCE
WHAT I COULD'VE DONE WITHOUT	PERSONAL CHARACTERISTICS AND STRENGTHS I DREW ON

PEOPLE I WORKED WITH (Place a ⊕ for a positive relationship, ⊖ for a negative relationship, or leave blank)

IF I COULD GO BACK IN TIME AND DO ONE THING DIFFERENTLY, IT WOULD BE…

ADDITIONAL COMMENTS

Work/Life Experiences 3/3

EXPERIENCE	DATE(S)

BRIEF DESCRIPTION OF THE EXPERIENCE

ACCOMPLISHMENTS (including any special recognition or awards if applicable)

ONE CHALLENGE I HAD TO NAVIGATE	WHAT I LIKED ABOUT THIS EXPERIENCE
WHAT I COULD'VE DONE WITHOUT	PERSONAL CHARACTERISTICS AND STRENGTHS I DREW ON

PEOPLE I WORKED WITH (Place a ⊕ for a positive relationship, ⊖ for a negative relationship, or leave blank)

IF I COULD GO BACK IN TIME AND DO ONE THING DIFFERENTLY, IT WOULD BE...

ADDITIONAL COMMENTS

My Career Wheel: Work/Life Experiences

Putting it all together

1. List your top three work or life experiences on the wheel section below.

2. Add any additional information learned to other appropriate wheel sections as needed.

Digging deeper

Similar to your learning experiences, looking at your top work/life experiences can help you begin to also identify patterns and learn about the conditions that are important for you to be able to do your best work. Some jobs may not have all of the qualities you identify, but understanding this can prepare you to advocate for yourself in the workplace, and recognize when opportunities are (or are not) a good fit, and why.

Career Opportunities

As you think about career opportunities, weigh your options and seek out new possibilities. Reviewing the map of your environment in the Significant Others section of this workbook may be a good place to start.

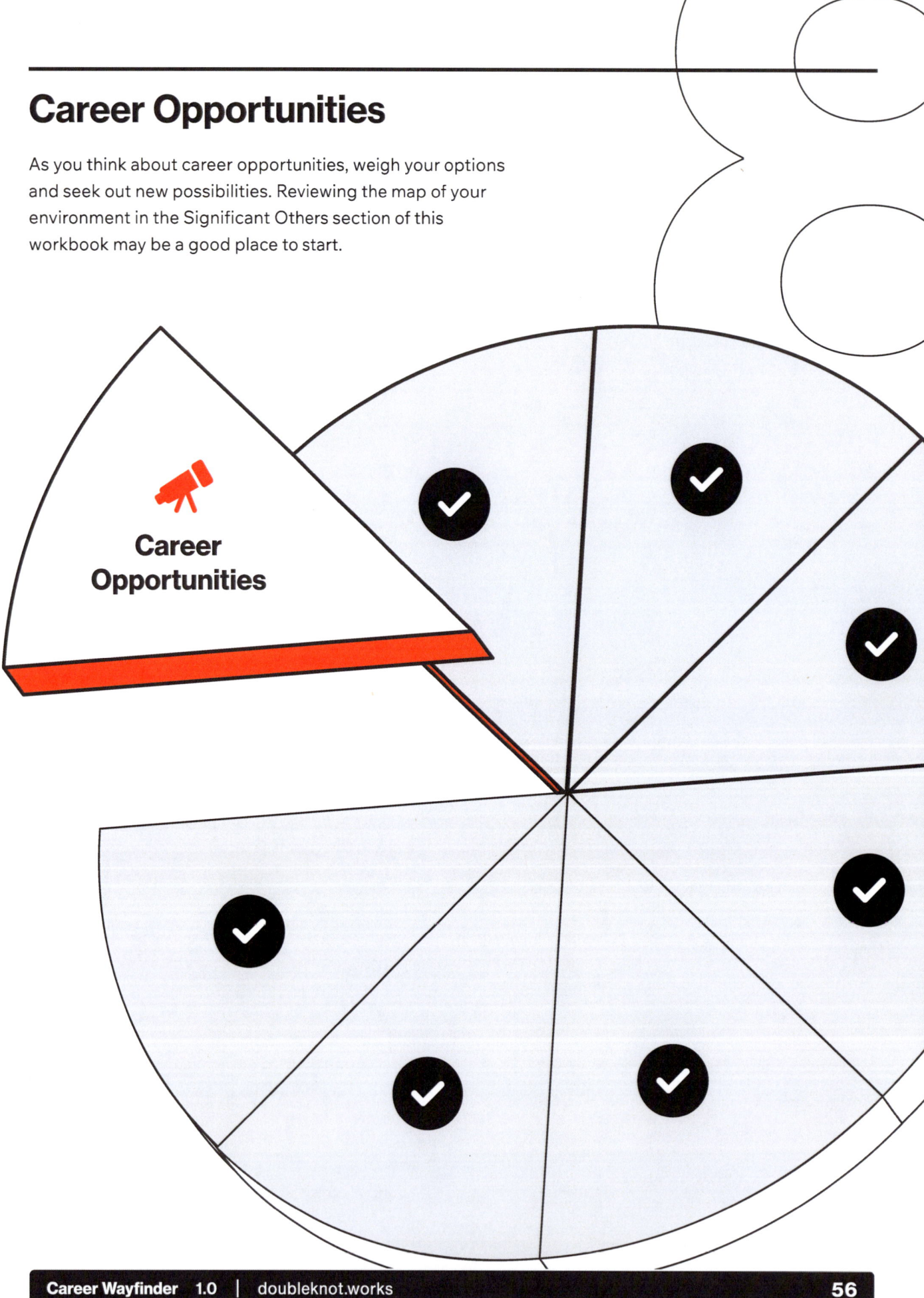

Career Opportunities

Expanding my network

Here are a few groups of connections you may want to consider.

Personal networking

Think about the people you know, and the people they might know. Whether you are actively looking for a job, or hoping to grow your career within your organization, letting others know what you are looking for will multiply the number of people supporting your next steps. You may also want to seek opportunities to connect and build relationships with people who are working in the area in which you are interested. Doing this in a genuine way will grow your network, as well as create natural opportunities for you to learn from others about openings of which you were not already aware.

Internal opportunities

You may already be working in a career, have a part-time job, or be volunteering. You may discover a new career trajectory within the company for which you are already working, or may be able to develop your skills in preparation for a career transition. Pay attention to what is happening around you, and do not be afraid to talk to your manager about future opportunities and your career development.

Labour market research

Information can be gathered about the labour market and general employment trends from a variety or sources. Doing your research and being aware of what is happening in the world will help you identify areas where future career opportunities might become available. This information can be discovered online, but may also be found in conversation with others and in the world around you, as you listen, discuss, and notice what is happening close to you. Research, and pay attention, and see what you can learn.

Career Opportunities

Brainstorming options

Do your research, and brainstorm some career opportunities that you might be interested in exploring. Review your career wheel sections, and place a star next to the five best opportunities.

My Career Wheel: Career Opportunities

Putting it all together

Write your top 5 career possibilities in this section of the wheel. Remember, these possibilities are giving you a place to start. As you learn more and explore, the options you list can be refined and adjusted as you go.

Digging deeper

Career opportunities (and possibilities) can change. If you get stuck, you may find it helpful to revisit the work you have done, and enlist the help of your career coach. Spend time doing some research, but remember that this list is a starting point that can change. Clarifying why something is not an option can also be helpful when trying to identify what your next step should be.

NOTES

03

Using my Career Wheel

Gaining Clarity

Using the career wheel as an organizing structure

The Career Wheel is a tool that can help you understand your strengths. It will help you organize and clarify information about yourself and who you are, as well as identify next steps forward, career options, and goals. The Career Wheel presents eight essential areas in career planning (skills, interests, values, personal style, significant others, learning experiences, work and life experience, and career opportunities). In the following chapters, you will work through a series of activities designed to help you understand yourself from the perspective of each section. Together, the eight sections of the wheel provide a more holistic perspective of who you are and the assets you have that will support your career development and decision-making process.

Though the Career Wheel is shown in this book as being divided into equal sections, some of the sections of the wheel may be more, or less, important in your life. The dotted lines allow you to re-draw the lines, changing the size of each section to reflect the areas that are more, or less, important to you.

Defining My Career Wheel

Take a moment to reflect on what your unique career wheel should look like, and re-draw where the dotted lines are to reflect who you are today and what is important to you. Some sections of the wheel may be more important in your decision-making than others.

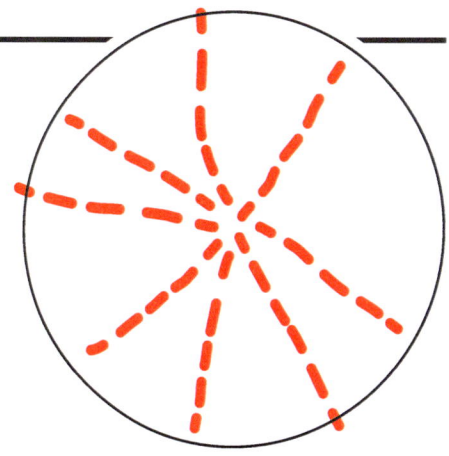

EXAMPLE

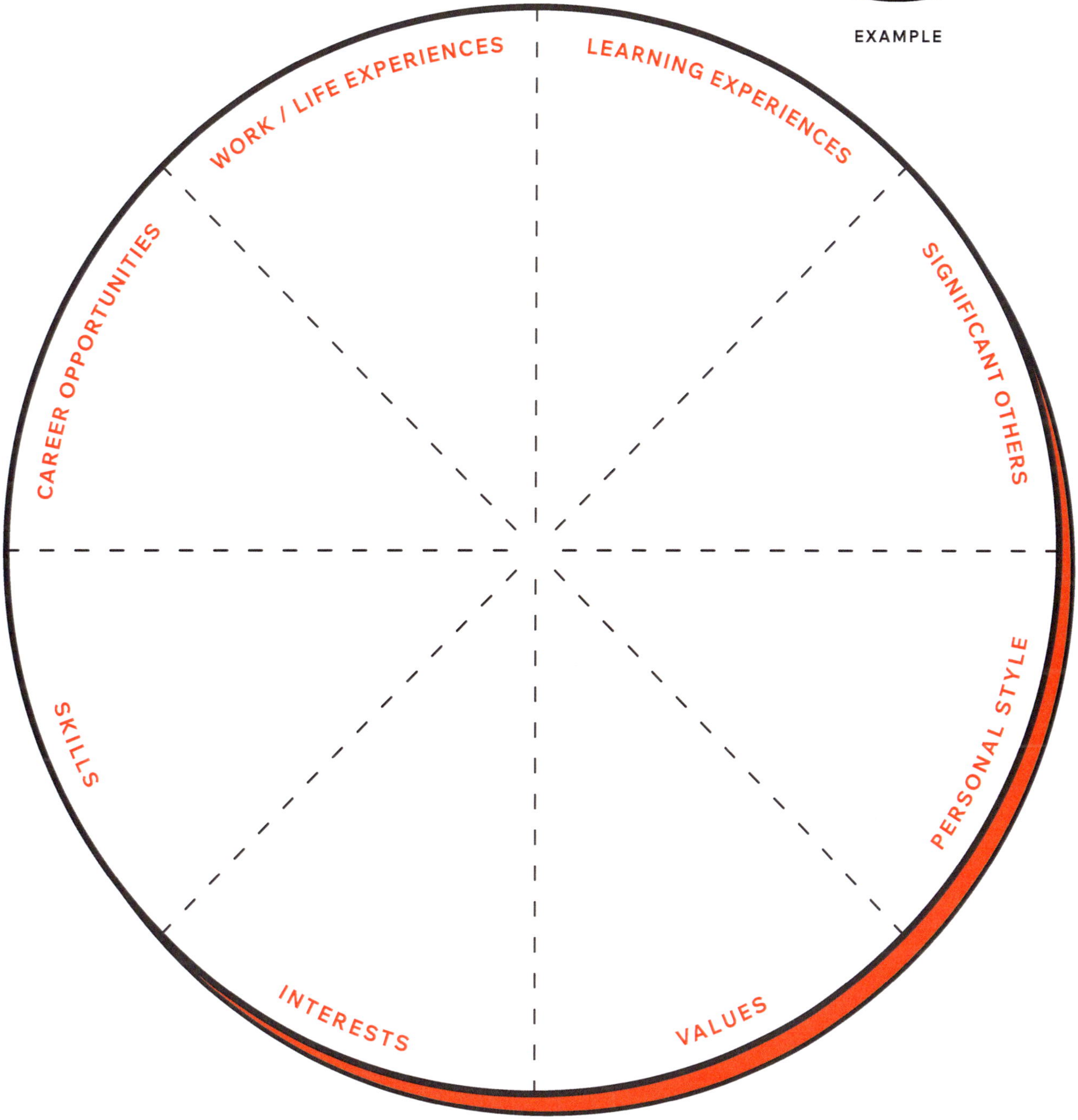

WORK / LIFE EXPERIENCES
LEARNING EXPERIENCES
CAREER OPPORTUNITIES
SIGNIFICANT OTHERS
SKILLS
PERSONAL STYLE
INTERESTS
VALUES

My Career Wheel

Review the activities you completed in the previous chapters. Write your name in the centre of the wheel, then fill in each section with the important information you want to remember. When you can, try limiting what you add to five ideas, to help you clarify what is most important.

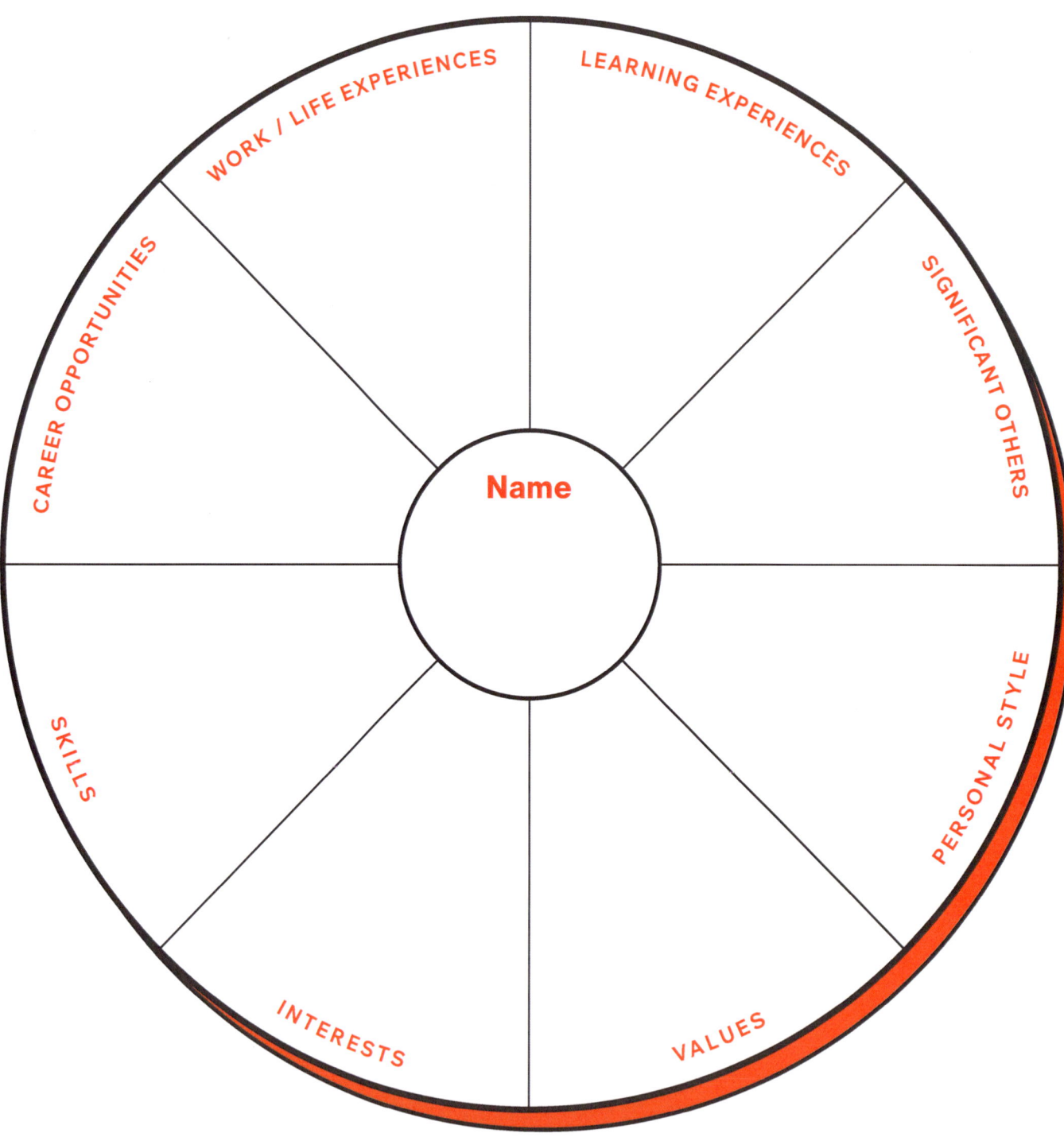

My Career Option Wheel

Now that you have filled out your career wheel, you can use the career decision-making wheel on the next page to help you organize information and make a decision about potential career options. Using the Career Option Wheel worksheet, place a possible career option in the centre of the wheel. Work your way around the wheel, filling in each section with the appropriate skills, interests, etc. for that option.

Once completed, compare the Career Option Wheel to your personal Career Wheel to see how this option fits for you. You may find you need to do this several times as different options arise. Here are a few questions to consider in each segment:

Work & Life Experiences

What previous work/life experience is needed?

What kinds of work/life experiences are sought after in this field?

Learning Experiences

What education is needed?

What opportunities for learning are available? (mentorship, pro-d, etc.)

Career Opportunities

Where might I find job openings?

Is this an industry that is growing/decreasing as a career?

What are the opportunities for career growth?

Significant Others

How would this career impact the significant others in your life?

Skills

What are the job-specific skills required for this work?

What transferable skills are important for this work?

Personal Style

What personal styles would be helpful in this type of work?

Interests

What interests do people typically have?

Values

What common values might people hold?

Exploring a Career Option 1/3

Place a possible career option in the centre of the wheel. Work your way around the wheel, filling in each segment with the appropriate skills, interests, etc. for that option.

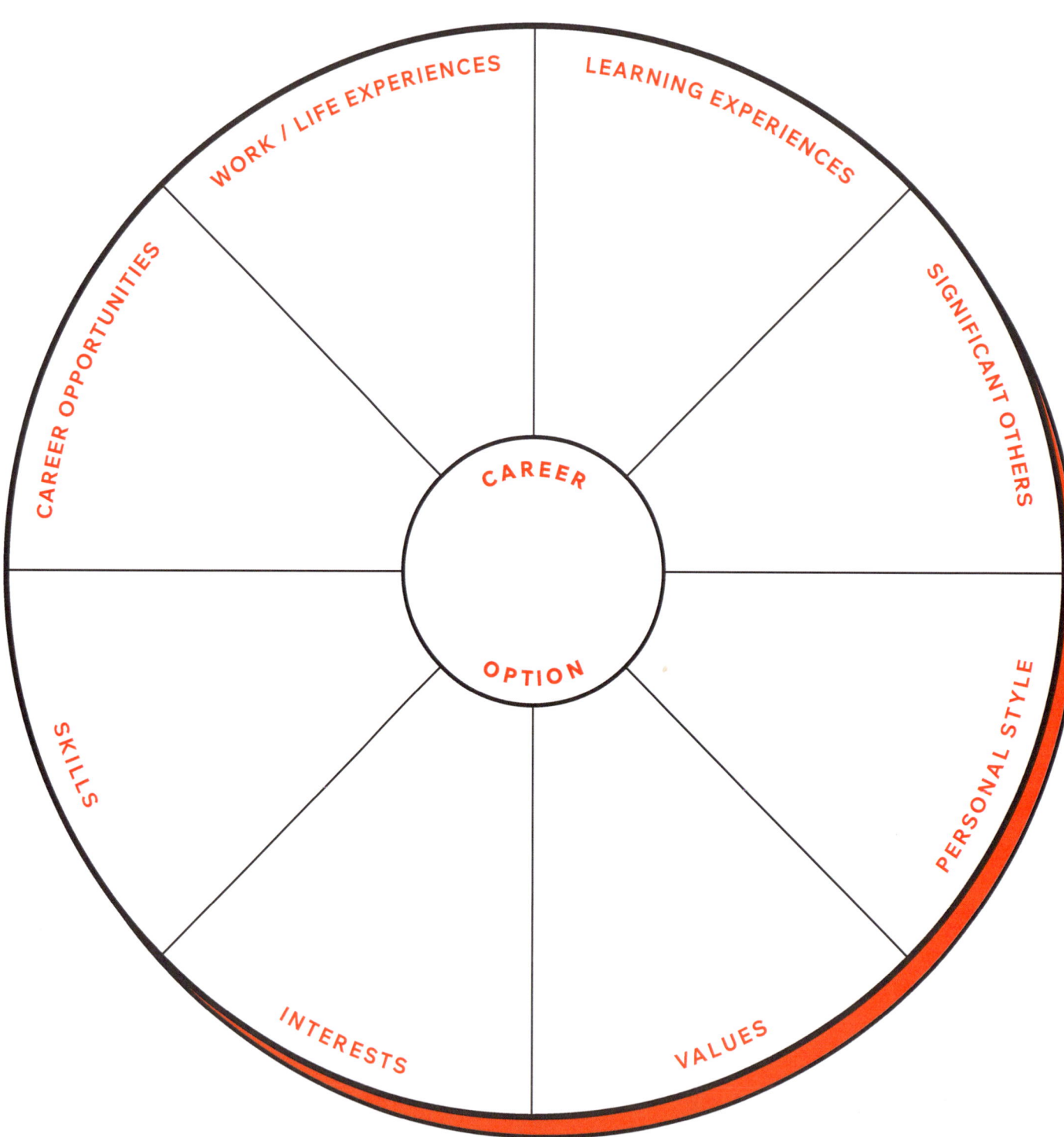

Exploring a Career Option

2/3

Place a possible career option in the centre of the wheel. Work your way around the wheel, filling in each segment with the appropriate skills, interests, etc. for that option.

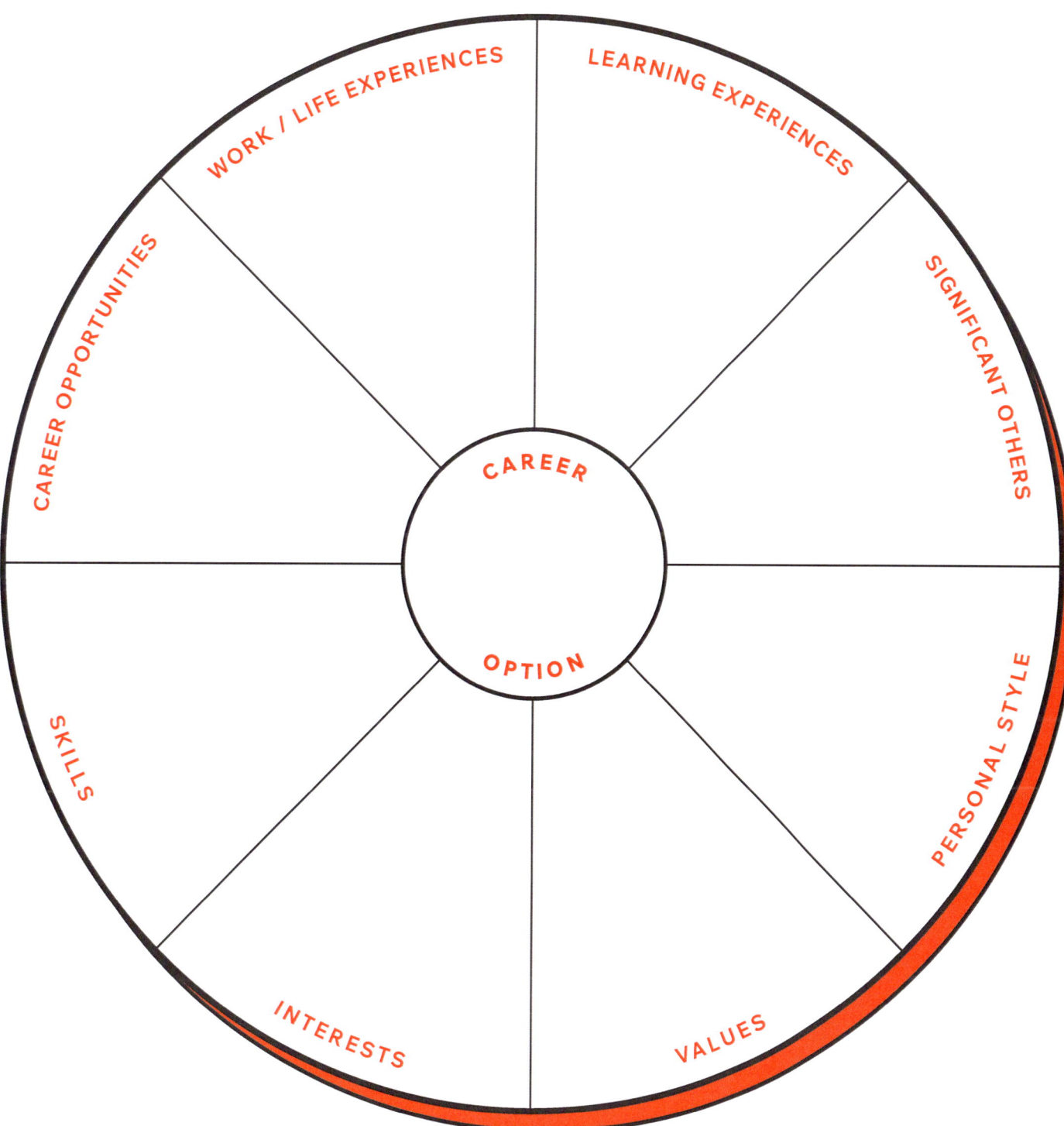

Exploring a Career Option

3/3

Place a possible career option in the centre of the wheel.
Work your way around the wheel, filling in each segment with the appropriate skills, interests, etc. for that option.

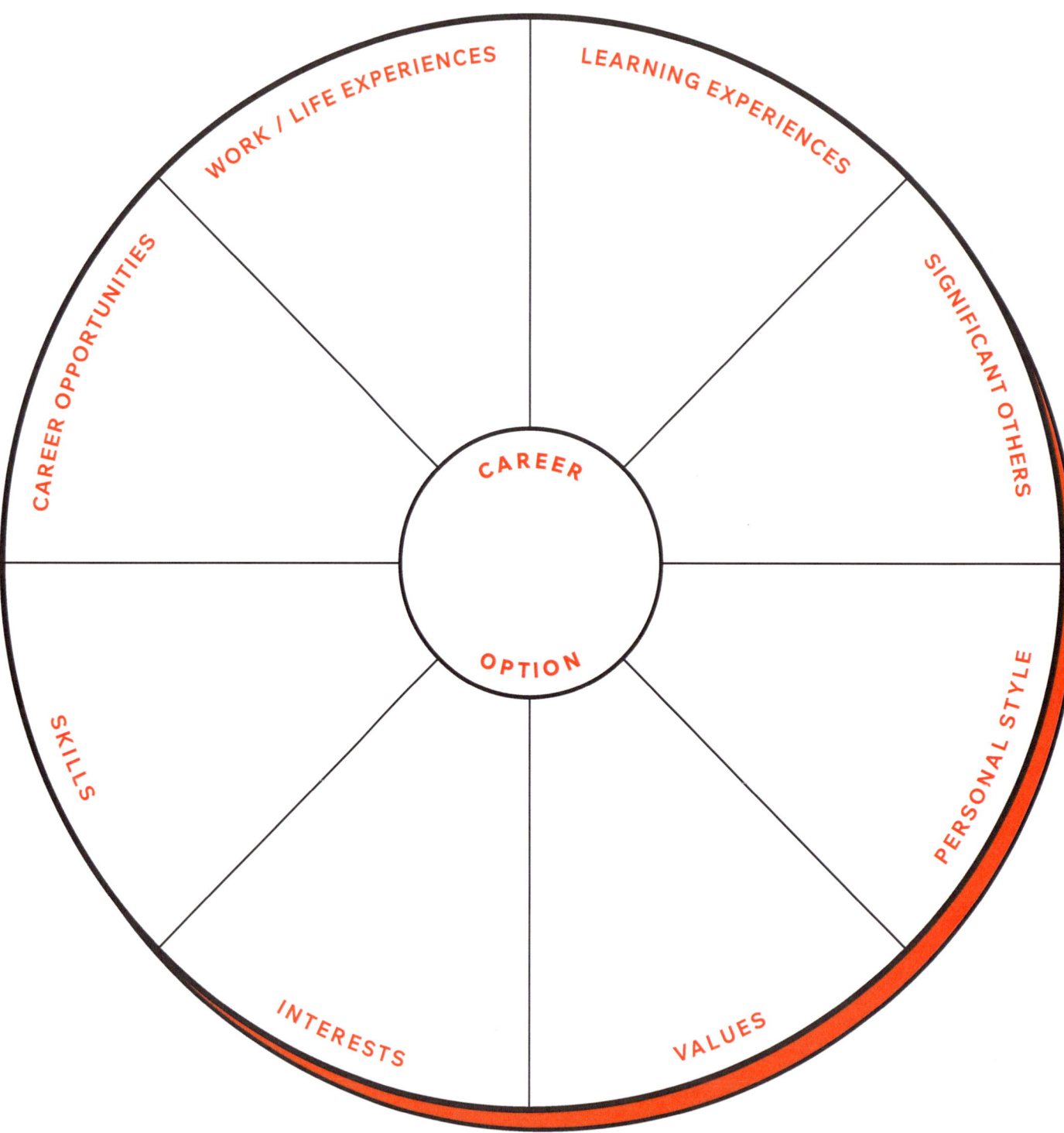

Career Wayfinder 1.0 | doubleknot.works

Informational Interviews

To find out more about a career option you are considering, talk to people who are already doing the work. This is called an informational interview, and it can help you learn more about what this option is actually like, while simultaneously expanding your network. When meeting with someone, remember that you are not asking for a job; you are only gathering information, and learning about the work they do and the industry in which they are working.

There are also lots of informational interview resources online, including lists of questions you might ask. Be mindful of the time you have, and what information will help you gain clarity as you make decisions.

Here are some sample questions to get you started.

General/Industry

- What are the typical duties of a person in this type of position?
- How do most people get into this kind of work?
- What are the ideal qualifications for someone in this field?
- What knowledge or skills are necessary for this work?
- What type of training or experience would be helpful for a person entering this field?
- Are there any specific courses I could take that would help me move into this career area?
- Can you give me an idea of the career paths available within this industry?
- What could I expect are the opportunities for advancement?
- Are there any similar types of jobs or related fields?
- What is the salary range for a _____ position within the industry?

Company

- What is the work environment here like?
- What qualities do you look for in new employees?
- How would you describe your company culture?

Personal

- How did you get started in this line of work?
- Do you know of anyone else that I could speak to?
- What advice would you give someone who wants to get into this field?

Informational Interview Planning 1/2

CAREER OPTION

NAME OF THE PERSON I'M INTERVIEWING

THEIR ROLE

ORGANIZATION

QUESTIONS I HAVE

During your interview you will want to take notes so you can compare what you learn as you interview people.

Give yourself some time following the interview to record your thoughts on your conversation. What stood out to you? Are there any notes or recommendations on which you want to take action? Also, how do you feel about how it went? What did you do well, and what would you do differently next time?

Informational Interview Planning 2/2

CAREER OPTION	
NAME OF THE PERSON I'M INTERVIEWING	THEIR ROLE
ORGANIZATION	

QUESTIONS I HAVE

_____
_____
_____
_____
_____
_____
_____
_____
_____
_____
_____
_____
_____
_____

Saying thank you goes a long way after an informational interview, and will help you make a lasting impression.

Take a few minutes after your informational interview to send a personalized note to the person you met with. Be specific, share what you appreciated about your conversation, and an invitation to stay in touch. Be professional, and genuine in your thanks. Try to send your note the same day as your interview.

NOTES

04

Looking forward & back

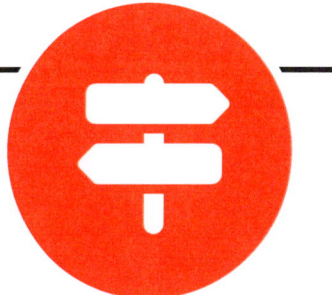

Goal-Setting & Planning

The journey continues

In this last section we focus on imagination, the path that has already been completed, and your ability to move through problems and life situations to consider what might lie ahead. This is a time for "possibility" thinking, a time to stretch your perspective. It is important not to minimize what you have achieved, and to set your vision on your hopes and dreams.

To assist you with this "stretching" process, you will be guided through liminal space. We will ask you to consider your life as a book, identifying the chapters you have already lived and the chapters still to be lived. The Vantage Point exercise shifts perspective and moves forward and backwards in time.

To conclude your wayfinding, you need to start with a plan of action and a determination of what needs to happen to take that first step. Taking action builds hope! Through action you gain momentum, and to keep that going it is helpful to have support and accountability along the way.

This Wayfinding workbook is only the start of your career journey, of which you are the captain and hopefully now better able to direct and find your way through still and turbulent waters.

Liminal space: Crossing through

Liminality is a place for creativity and learning to emerge. Moments of pause in liminal space can provide the opportunity to see what may not have previously been visible, creating the conditions needed to build something new. Here are a few strategies as you navigate your own liminal experience:

Resisting change

- **Understand what will cause you to react, rather than respond.** Emotions may surface unexpectedly or be particularly strong at the beginning of your entry into liminal space. Be aware of moments of resistance that may emerge.

- **You may feel the need to rush forward with an urgency to just do something.** It can be tempting to try to fill the space of uncertainty without knowing what that space needs or what the next step is.

- **Feelings of frustration or anger may emerge.** These feelings may be directed at others or the system you are (or were) navigating, resulting in your moving into a position of attack.

Understanding yourself in change

- **Embrace your vulnerability, challenges, and moments of not knowing.** These provide opportunities for you to learn and grow.

- **Get to know yourself.** Clarify what you believe to be true, your values, and who you are. Trust you have something of value to contribute, and work on letting go of habits that are not serving you well.

- **Be courageous.** Do not get caught up in the expectations of others, or prioritize their praise as a measure of success more valuable than your own contentment. Pay attention to that small inner voice.

As you navigate this uncertainty, there can be moments of wanting to turn back to the familiar (even if it is not a good option) or settling for something less than what you had hoped for, but is easy. As you engage in this process, our hope is that something new will emerge for you, while also acknowledging the journey you have been on.

My Career Story

Imagine your life is a book. What would the title be? What would the big idea of your book be? If you look back and break up your life into chapters, what would those be? **Use these prompts to reflect further on who you are, and the journey you are on.**

MY NAME	
BOOK TITLE	

DEDICATION	COVER

CHAPTER TITLES	
1	
2	
3	
4	
5	

LESSONS LEARNED IN EACH CHAPTER	
1	
2	
3	
4	
5	

My Career Story CONTINUED

Your story is not over! See if you can identify two or three future chapters that are still to be written. **What are a few steps you might take in those chapters?**

CHAPTER TITLE

POSSIBLE STEPS I MIGHT TAKE TO MAKE THIS CHAPTER A REALITY

CHAPTER TITLE

POSSIBLE STEPS I MIGHT TAKE TO MAKE THIS CHAPTER A REALITY

CHAPTER TITLE

POSSIBLE STEPS I MIGHT TAKE TO MAKE THIS CHAPTER A REALITY

Visioning to gain perspective

Vantage Points is a visualization exercise that creates opportunities for you to gain new perspectives on a challenge. As you follow the prompts listed and move through the space, your movement and the space you are in create a metaphor for the challenge you are exploring. **Follow the prompts below, working through them with a coach or on your own.**

Vantage Points Activity

- Stand up in the middle of the room.

- Feel the ground beneath your feet, and take a breath.

- Think about where you are at, and how you are feeling today.

- Now, bring to mind a challenge you are facing. It may be an actual challenge, or may be an area of your life where you are feeling uncertain and do not know how you would like to proceed...

- Thinking about this uncertainty, look across the room, and imagine the side of the room you are looking at represents what the perfect outcome of the challenge you have in mind might be, or how it would feel.

- When you are ready, walk to the other side of the room and stand in that perfect ending you are imagining.

- You have made it! Pause here and notice – how does it feel?

- Take a moment and look back at where you were standing. What do you notice looking back at where you once stood? From where you are standing now, what advice do you want to give that version of yourself? What do you need to hear? (Pause and notice.)

- When you are ready, walk back to the centre of the room. As you walk, reflect on what exists in the space between where you are today, and your perfect ending. There may be barriers or challenges blocking your way. It may feel foggy, or perhaps there is a different path to be taken. What do you notice?

- Who else is walking this path with you? Is there more than one way to make it to the other side? What else is there that may not have been seen previously? How big/small is the barrier? Is it a barrier? You may have had to walk around a chair, or perhaps step over something. Use what is around you to help expand the metaphor of this space.

Visioning to gain perspective CONTINUED

- You began by standing in the middle of the room. Now, standing back at that middle-point, turn around and look behind you.

- How far have you come? What have you already accomplished to be standing here today? How much uncertainty and challenge have you already navigated? What strengths have you already demonstrated? Is there anything you have been carrying that you wish to leave behind?

- Looking back at what you have already navigated provides evidence from which strengths can be identified. Strengths can be drawn on in support of forward movement and whatever the next step might be.

- Turn around and look back across the room, towards the place that represented your perfect ending. What do you notice? As you start thinking about heading towards that perfect ending once again, it all starts with just one step.

- Sometimes identifying a first step is not what is actually needed, and there is something happening below the surface that must be addressed in order to be successful. Looking back at the Hope-Action Theory, your self-reflection, self-clarity, and visioning are important areas to spend time on before setting goals and putting plans into action. Slow down, and see if you can identify what is at the root of the challenge on which you are focusing.

- If we examine that first step a little more closely, you will notice that it starts with shifting and rebalancing, lifting your leg and swinging it forward. Is there something that needs to happen before that first step is taken?

- Or, maybe we need to think about the first step as a pivot point. Uncertainty can come from any direction. With your foot planted, it becomes an anchor point, strengthening your position and preparing you to pivot (or absorb impact) as needed. How might you strengthen this anchor point and prepare yourself for a possible pivot?

- Is there anything else? Return to your seat, and pause to reflect on this experience.

- What have you learned? Where have you made progress?

Getting ready to make a plan

You have learned about who you are from a range of perspectives, moving from Self-Reflection to imagining possibilities. The next step is to develop a plan and identify some goals to help you continue to grow.

Take a moment to look back to where you were when you started this workbook.

Activity

Thinking back to where you were at at the beginning of this workbook, where have you made progress?

_____
_____
_____

What have you learned about who you are?

_____
_____
_____
_____

What specifically have you learned about your personal career development?

_____
_____
_____

Developing a plan of action can feel hard, and not worth your time or effort. It is, however, important to develop a plan that is uniquely tailored to who you are, setting you up for success in the future.

Developing your plan with the support of a certified coach will help to make sure you have an effective plan, and will provide you with the support you need beyond the pages of this workbook.

Developing my plan

Recognizing where you are today and the knowledge that you have, look ahead and think about where you would like to be. As you prepare to implement the goals and plans you have made, take some time to first build a stronger foundation for these plans.

Activity

What is one thing I can commit to doing to continue moving forward?

_____

Break down your plan into smaller actions below. What specifically do you need to do, or be aware of, to successfully put your plan into action?

- First, I need to…

  _____

- Then, I will…

  _____

- After that I will…

  _____

- Something I need to pay attention to and don't want to forget is…

  _____

What will change for you when you implement your plan?

_____

What will the impact be on the people around you?

_____

Accountability

You know yourself and what you need to actually implement the plans you have outlined. It can be easy to start strong, but lose momentum over time as other things get in the way or become distractions. The more specific you can be in your responses, the better. Some people find booking time in their calendar helpful. Others find it helpful to share their plans with someone, and have them serve as an accountability partner.

Activity

What do you need, to make sure you follow through on the plans you have made?

- A sign that I'm losing focus on my plan will be…

- The resources I can access to help me put my plan into action are…

- The strengths I have that will help me maintain my momentum are…

- The people in my life that can provide me with resources and support as I implement my plan are…

NAME	HOW THEY CAN HELP
NAME	HOW THEY CAN HELP
NAME	HOW THEY CAN HELP

The person I will share my plan with and ask them to help me stay accountable is…

If my plan needs to change, the person I will talk to for support and help adapting is…

Congratulations!

You have completed Career Wayfinder and your personal career wheel.

Take a moment to think back to the day you started working through this workbook. What have you learned about who you are?

It is important to note that throughout your life, your wheel will change as you have new experiences, continue to learn, and develop your career.

As you continue to take steps, it is important to stay positive, even in the midst of uncertainty. Continue to work on building forward momentum, even when the path may seem unclear. Doors may open unexpectedly, and you will be glad to have done this work to be prepared for these new opportunities.

You may also encounter unexpected challenges. Think back to the Hope-Action Theory introduced at the beginning of this book. Hope is not just feeling positive, it is a deeper understanding that there is more to life and the work you do. The exercises you have completed throughout this workbook are some of the strategies you might use to increase your sense of hope.

Continue learning about who you are, connecting with the people around you, trusting yourself to find your way forwards, and then courageously step into the work that you are uniquely called to do.

Completing this workbook will help with the first part of the journey you are undertaking, but there is more work to be done. Hopefully you are now in a position where you have some goals, and perhaps a plan for how to get started. You may need to brush up on your job search skills, and for that we can recommend an online resource called *Job Search Strategies*. You also will need to implement the plan you have devised. Hopefully this will work out fine, but some flexibility and adaptation may also be needed. In responding to changes in direction, you will find it helpful to go back to the work you have completed in this workbook. The need for reflection, clarity, and visioning is ongoing.

We wish you well on your career life journey!

Acknowledgements

A workbook such as this builds on input from many people.

We want to start by thanking Dr. Spencer Niles. You have made a significant contribution through your work on Hope-Action Theory and the "Life as a Book" exercise. We are grateful for many opportunities to collaborate with you through speaking engagements and the *Hope-Action Theory and Practice* certification program. Our shared projects have provided us with fertile ground for exploring some of the interventions that are included in this workbook. Gray Poehnell, thank you for contributing to the *Career Pathways* and *Guiding Circles* programs. In some respects, this workbook is an updated and expanded version of these earlier programs and the projects worked on over the years.

As a daughter-father writing team, family has always been important in our lives. This has also been the case in the writing of this book, which has in many ways been a family project. We are so grateful to be able to work together, finding joy in the work we share with our family.

Jenna Amundson, we are so grateful for your work on this book. Your expert input surpassed that of an editor. Your attention to detail combined with your experience working with women and youth provided a solid foundation for the questions you asked, and the insights you offered. Your ability to see the details and help us clarify what was being said was tremendously helpful.

Nick Fruhling, thank you for sharing our excitement and vision for this book. The way you communicate meaning through design has turned this book into a work of art. This workbook wouldn't be what it is today without your commitment to quality, and your relentless pursuit of delight in all of life.

Jeanette Amundson, you have been a constant supporter, and foundation for our family. Long before the ideas in this book were ever imagined, your wisdom and encouragement helped us all become who we are today. Thank you for your ongoing support, and the ways you love and care for our family.

We want to acknowledge the unceded territory of the Musqueam people located near the historical Musqueam camps of q̓ʷeyaʔχʷ (Garry Point), on whose land we are honoured to teach, learn, and live. Traditionally and ancestrally, and since the beginning of memory, the hən̓q̓əmin̓əm̓ speaking Musqueam people have shared the stewardship of this land, located at the mouth of a great river (stó:lō) with Tsawassen, Kwantlen, and other Coast Salish Peoples.

This land was once used as a place to gather, and collect resources such as berries, salmon, and more. We hope that this book will serve as another type of resource from which our readers can grow and thrive.

We would like to encourage you, the reader, to reflect on your journey with this workbook. You have your own family history, stories, location, and circumstances that have brought you to this point. As you complete this workbook, take a moment to list the people who have supported you and for whom you are thankful. Your own stories and writing have enriched this workbook, and we are grateful for your active and ongoing participation.

_____

_____

_____

_____

_____

_____

_____

_____

_____

About the Authors

Andrea Fruhling PCC

Andrea is a Certified Organizational Coach, the Founding Director of Doubleknot Works, a Mentor Coach & Instructor for the University of British Columbia's Organizational Coaching certification program, the developer and lead instructor for the Career Coaching Masterclass (UBC), and expert trainer for the internationally attended Certification in Hope-Action Theory & Practice. Andrea leads the International Coaching Federation's Career Coaching Community of Practice, and is a certified facilitator in the LEGO® Serious Play® Methodology.

Andrea develops and delivers training and group coaching programs for coaches, industry leaders, and organizations, helping them find engaging and impactful ways to work with people, support career development, and increase hopefulness. She has delivered numerous keynote presentations and workshops for national and international conferences, career development associations, organizations, and a broad range of client groups. Her work is practical and engaging with a focus on creativity, active, strengths-based learning, team engagement, and hope.

Dr. Norman Amundson

Dr. Amundson is a professor emeritus from the University of British Columbia. He has a PhD from the University of Alberta and also holds an Honorary Doctorate from the University of Umea, Sweden. He has worked in the career development field for over 40 years. During this time he has published many books and articles, including a 2018 Anniversary Edition of his nationally award-winning book *Active Engagement*. Most recently he has co-authored the books *Career Flow & Development: Hope in Action* and *Career Recovery: Creating Hopeful Careers in Difficult Times*. Many of his books and workbooks have been translated into other languages (Japanese, Korean, Danish, Swedish, Finnish, French, Latvian, Estonian, Romanian, Icelandic, Arabic, Hungarian, Polish, Greek, Dutch).

In his work, he emphasizes the importance of creativity, imagination, storytelling, dynamic action, metaphors, and hope. Dr. Amundson has presented his work at many national and international conferences (in more than 30 countries) and has been recognized by many national and international professional associations for his leadership and contributions in the career development field. His training workshops and presentations are practical, engaging, and interactive.

References & Resources

Hope-Action Theory and Hope-Action Inventory Assessment
Developed in 2010 by Dr. Spencer Niles, Dr. Hyung Joon Yoon, and Dr. Norm Amundson
Additional references and resources available at https://hopeactioninventory.com

Liminal Space
The Experience of Liminal Space: https://bit.ly/Liminal1
Liminal Space in Career Conversations: https://bit.ly/liminal2

Metaphor Map: Full colour printable available at: https://doubleknot.works/resources

The Career Wheel: Amundson, N.E. (1989). A model of individual career counseling. *Journal of Employment Counseling*, 26(3), 146-152.

My Life as a Book: Niles, S. G., Amundson, N. E. & Neault, R. A. (2010). *Career flow: A hope-centered approach to career development*. Boston, MA: Pearson Education.

Vantage Points: Adaptation of 'Walking the Problem'
Amundson, N. E. (1998). *Active engagement: Enhancing the career counselling process*. Richmond, BC: Ergon Communications.

Career Pathways: Amundson, N.E., & Poehnell, G. (2004). *Career pathways* (3rd ed.). Richmond, BC: Ergon Communications.

Career Flow & Development: Hope in Action: Niles, S., Amundson, N.E., Neault, R., & Yoon, H.J. (2021). *Career flow & development: Hope in action*. San Diego, CA: Cognella.

Job Search Strategies

Access our Job Search Strategies course online at: https://doubleknot.works/job-search

Colophon

Career Wayfinder uses the typefaces Neue Haas Grotesk and Wix Madefor for text, Font Awesome for iconography, and BC Sans to represent the hən̓q̓əmin̓əm̓ language.

BC Sans 2.0 is a font designed to support special characters and syllabics found in Indigenous Languages. With the participation of the Government of British Columbia, this modified version of Noto Sans was developed and released under an open-source license for public use.

This book was proudly planned, designed, edited, and produced in Figma.

www.ingramcontent.com/pod-product-compliance
Lightning Source LLC
Chambersburg PA
CBRC101309020426
42333CB00009B/80